You Make My Heart Giggle

Dadisms

The Wisdom and Wit of Dad

Recorded by a grateful son
Brent John Larsen

YOU MAKE MY HEART GIGGLE
Dadisms, The Wisdom and Wit of Dad

LARSEN, BRENT JOHN, Author
YOU MAKE MY HEART GIGGLE
BRENT JOHN LARSEN

Published by:
ELITE ONLINE PUBLISHING
63 East 11400 South
Suite #230
Sandy, UT 84070
EliteOnlinePublishing.com

ISBN: 978-1-961801-73-8 (Paperback)
ISBN: 978-1-961801-74-5 (Audiobook)
ISBN: 978-1-961801-75-2 (eBook)

BIO006000
FAM033000

Edited by Mary DoRooa

QUANTITY PURCHASES: Schools, companies, professional groups, clubs, and other organizations may qualify for special terms when ordering quantities of this title.
For information, email info@eliteonlinepublishing.com.

TABLE OF CONTENTS

INTRODUCTION ix

CHAPTER 1

"Faint heart never won fair maiden." 1

John Wesley Powell, intrepid Grand Canyon and Colorado
River explorer

Courage / Determination

CHAPTER 2

"Until my doings catch up with my knowings, I ain't got
time for new learnin's" 9

Apollo moon landing, one of the most incredible
achievements in human history

Education / Learning

CHAPTER 3

"Be a member of the construction crew, and not
a member of the wrecking gang." 19

Dads journal entries from World War II in the
Pacific Theater

Positive Influence / Making a Difference

CHAPTER 4

"A Larsen can do anything" 31

The Wright Brothers, first powered flight —
Ingenuity and perseverance that changed the world

Optimism

CHAPTER 5

"It's a cinch by the inch, and a trial by the mile" 43

Building of the Transcontinental Railroad and
"Hell on Wheels"

Patience / Perspective

CHAPTER 6

"You can't make a silk purse out of a sow's ear...or
can you?" 53

Walt Disney, a creative visionary who gave us "The Happiest
Place on Earth"

Creativity

CHAPTER 7

"Bring on another mountain." 63

Ernest Shackelton, the greatest story of human survival
against all odds

Opposition / Growth

CHAPTER 8

"Take care of the corners and the middle will take care
of its self" 75

D-Day invasion, the largest, and most complex military
operation in history. Normandy France, World War II

Attention to Small Details

CHAPTER 9

"Just get back up one more time." 83

Thomas Edison, one of the most prolific inventors
of all time (light bulb to phonograph)

Tenacity / Endurance

CHAPTER 10

"Don't get in a pissing contest with a skunk.". 91

Mark Twain, a colorful and beloved American author

Wisdom / Restraint

CHAPTER 11

"Have a hap, hap, happy day!" 97

#1 song on the British BBC radio during the Battle of
Britain in World War II

Joy / Happiness

CHAPTER 12

"It's easier to gain forgiveness than permission." 103

Teddy Roosevelt, 26th U.S. President, reformer,
conservationist, and dynamic leader

Initiative

CHAPTER 13

"The sheep grow fat only under the shepherd's eye." 113

Steve Jobs, visionary who created Apple Inc,
one of the most successful companies ever

Vision

CHAPTER 14

"Message to Garcia" 127

The story behind the message

Dependability / Commitment

CHAPTER 15

"If it's worth doing, it's worth doing well." 135

George Pocock, known for building the finest racing
shells in the world

Excellence / Pride

CHAPTER 16

"He who dances, has to pay the fiddler. Or pay the
fiddler, and then the dance is yours." 141

The Beatles, considered the greatest rock band with
20 #1 singles

Accountability / Hard Work

CHAPTER 17

"No empty chairs" 149

Rescue of shipwrecked sailors in Scheveningen
Holland

Priorities / Relationships

CHAPTER 18

"That which we persist in doing becomes easier" 157

Panama Canal, the greatest engineering feat
in the world

Persistence / Goals

CHAPTER 19

"Just add another cup of water to the soup."...........165

"We band of brothers" St Crispin's Day speech from
Shakespeare's play *Henry V*

Friendship / Inclusion

CHAPTER 20

"Call a Spade a Spade"..........................173

Bonanza silver mine and the wild west town of Frisco

Honesty / Truthfulness

CHAPTER 21

"My word is my bond"...........................179

The Go-Getter — a story written by Peter Kyne that
tells you how to be one

Integrity

CHAPTER 22

"My sweetheart is my queen and will be treated like one.". . 189

"The Letter" — from Sullivan Ballou to his wife just before
his death in the Civil War

Love / Respect

About the Author...............................197

Visit YouMakeMyHeartGiggle.com
for resources and more.

INTRODUCTION

THERE IS A GENTLE tapping on the front door followed by the turning of the knob and a timid push. Through a small crack, a blond tassel of hair appears followed by two beautiful blue eyes that dance with excitement and a little bit of mischief. With his eyes sweeping the room to make sure the coast appears clear, the little explosion of energy bursts into the room. It is Andrew, he is six years old, and he is on a mission. He is to deliver a secret message that no one but the old man has security clearance to see. He soon locates his objective and climbs up onto Grandpa's lap. There is, of course, "the secret code" to authenticate that this is the right Grandpa. It comes in the form of a big bear hug. And once Andrew receives it, he knows he has found his intended target. The secret envelope is then opened to reveal the highly sensitive message inside. It reads: "I love coming to Grandpa's house because you make my heart giggle." A few tears well up in the old man's eyes, and a second hug is given to simply say, "Message received, and understood."

This secret message has caused me to reflect on the importance of our heart in everything we do in life — especially those things that have real meaning. All of us can reflect on experiences that have forever altered the direction of our lives. Two life-altering events that happened to me both involved the heart. The first was where I honestly felt that my heart would break. It occurred with the death of my ten-year-old son, Eric, from a tragic drowning accident. The second was where my heart actually did break. It happened when I went into total cardiac arrest caused by cardiomyopathy: a condition where my heart muscle became so weak that it simply stopped working. The chance of my survival was around one percent. The chance of my son's survival was zero.

I have learned powerful lessons from these two experiences.

From Eric's death I sadly learned the importance of priorities.

From my own brush with death, I learned to be grateful.

Concerning the importance of gratitude, Michael J Fox, who has battled Parkinson's Disease for over thirty-two years, has said, "With gratitude, optimism is sustainable. And if you can find something to be grateful for, you can find something to look forward to, and you carry on." He has since raised over $2 billion for Parkinson's research to find a cure.

I wanted to share with others the lessons I have learned, not only from these two experiences, but also from my life as a whole. I have come to the realization that the best teachers have been those that I love the most. And one who stands out largely in my life is my father. I was a very ordinary son, but he was an extraordinary father.

Dad taught a lot of life's lessons through what I have come to call "Dadisms" — sayings that reminded me of stories he would use in order to teach me life's lessons.

Each chapter in this book begins with one of the Dadisms, followed by the principle(s) that Dad was trying to teach. I end each chapter with a story from history that teaches the same lesson. Each chapter stands independently of the others.

Life is made up of accumulated experiences. And I have chosen to tell them mostly in story form.

"Tell me facts and I will learn.
Tell me the truth and I will remember it.
Tell me a story and it will live in my heart forever."

Steve Sabol, NFL Films

I wanted to give some insight as to why the bond between fathers and sons exists. Not only as a son to my father, but also as a father to my sons. The lessons my father taught me were ones he learned in large part from his father, and the lessons my sons and grandsons are learning from me, came from Dad.

One day I ran across two journal entries — one from Charles Francis Adams, the other from his son, Brook. Charles was the son of John Quincy Adams, the seventh president of the United States, and the grandson of John Adams our second president. Charles was born in 1807 in Massachusetts, He had practiced law with Daniel Webster and had served as a state senator. He ran unsuccessfully for vice president in the election of 1848. He served as Lincoln's foreign minister to London during the Civil War and, in 1869, as an overseer at Harvard University. To say the least, he was a very busy man. Brook, his second oldest child, had hungered for any interaction with his busy father, and finally convinced his dad one day to take him fishing. Their journal entries of that activity are quite striking. Charlie's entry on that day read as follows: "Went fishing with my son today, a day wasted." Brook, his son, wrote in his journal that same day: "Went fishing with my father today — the most wonderful day of my life." I shed a tear when I read that passage. It was totally foreign to me that such a relationship could exist. My dad was my hero, my confidant and my best friend growing up.

We use such terms as:

"He's got heart."   Refers to passion

"Give it all your heart."   Means personal effort

"Heartfelt"	Relates to a sense of being genuine
"He broke my heart."	Love lost or disappointment
"Heartache"	Causing emotional pain
"Heartless"	Without feeling or affection

The heart is the symbol of love, and love is the most powerful force in the world. The Christians believe that the first and greatest commandment is to love God, and the second is like unto it, to love thy neighbor as thyself. The Muslims believe that God is so loving that he created His attribute of love as an instinct in us. Hence, true love is part of God's love. The Buddhists believe that love is a gift of one's innermost soul to another, so both can be whole.

A little about my dad:

Little Johnny, as my father was known, spent his early childhood in Cache Valley, a beautiful mountain setting in northern Utah. The valley was lush and green in summer with horses and cows grazing peacefully in fields framed by homemade log and wire fences. The severe winters were in stark contrast to the mild summers. Bitterly cold, but beautiful. Each morning, the sun would stream through the trees, causing the hoar frost (which had settled on the branches during the night) to sparkle like a thousand little gems. Against a cobalt blue sky, the contrast was stunning. Cache Valley was a wonderful place for an active young boy to grow up in; pine covered mountains to climb, clear running rivers to fish, and plenty of places to explore. Cache Valley got its name from the mountain men and trappers who traveled the Rockies in search of valuable furs, such as fox, beaver and bear. Beaver pelts were in high demand in the east because top hats were all the rage, and a beaver top hat signaled wealth and class. Jim Bridger and Jedediah Smith were a few of those who roamed the high mountains in the 1820s. Jedediah was born and raised in Boston, and Jim hailed from Chicago. These young men had left the comforts of eastern cities for the lonely and rugged life in the west. It was a solitary existence, always working the trap lines by themselves. Each spring, around the first week in May, these intrepid young men would come together to retrieve their hidden fur "caches" that they had created during the winter months in what was for them the high social event of the year. It was called "the rendezvous."

Dad's father, Rube, was slight of build. He had come from humble circumstances. Raised on a small farm that managed to put food on the table but little else, Rube would spend his entire life raising livestock and living off the land the same as his father and his grandfather before him had done. Dad's mother, Charlotte, was the daughter of John Anderson who was a tall man, and rather quiet and soft spoken. He was impeccable in appearance and altogether a rather handsome man. He had amassed a small fortune in real estate and as president of the Logan First National Bank and as the proprietor of the old ZCMI Mercantile Store on Main Street. His parents had walked from St Louis Missouri to the Rocky Mountains to homestead in the northern Utah territory in 1859, and John was born a few years later in 1864. It was said of Charlotte that she could have any man in the valley, but she settled on a quiet country boy. As a cattleman, Rube was hardly ever home. He was demanding of his children, but in a kind sort of way.

My father, Little Johnny, was a very active and outgoing young boy with little fear of anything, always towering over his fellow schoolmates. Despite his size, he was a kind and gentle child. As an adult, he was larger than life, not only physically, but also large intellectually, emotionally, and spiritually. At six foot six and 320 pounds, with size 16 shoes and a coat size 56, everyone quit calling him Little Johnny, and he simply became known as Big John.

He had an unwavering love for his country. He was part of what Tom Brokaw called "the Greatest Generation," serving in

World War II in the South Pacific. He was involved in the battles at Saipan, Tinian, Iwo Jima, Leyte, Philippines, and Okinawa, along with being part of one of the first contingencies to enter Hiroshima after the atomic bomb was dropped.

He loved golf, he loved to travel, and he never held public office, but was deeply involved in local caucuses, state conventions, and campaigning for candidates he believed in. As far as singing, he could not carry a tune, but he loved music and the arts and saw to it that we often attended the Utah Symphony, plays at the Promised Valley Playhouse, and excursions to the local galleries, so we could appreciate fine art. We could decide for ourselves as to whether or not we wanted to play sports, but we had no such freedom when it came to learning how to play a musical instrument. To Dad, it was non-negotiable. He said simply, "You will."

I knew he loved me, not only by what he said, but by what he actually did. One night in late August 1968, my father came home from work and asked if he could visit with me for a few minutes. My first though was, "Oh no, what have I done now?" I soon realized that his tone was very different from past visits. He said, "Son, I have been offered the job to be the principal of your high school, and I need to know if that would bother you in any way." I then asked him what he would do if the answer was yes. His response surprised me. He said, "Son, you are far more important than any job could ever be, and if it would cause you even the slightest worry or concern, I will turn the job down." I knew that he really wanted that job, but I also knew he really meant what he said. My answer to him was that it would be fine, and for the next three years we had what many would call a rather unique experience together.

I hope the stories I tell here will be of some interest. But more importantly I hope they will awaken in each reader the realization of the lessons that each has learned from those who have been their source of inspiration and learning. Those who have truly made a difference in their lives.

CHAPTER 1

"FAINT HEART NEVER WON FAIR MAIDEN (OR ANYTHING ELSE FOR THAT MATTER)"

Courage / Determination

"What lies ahead I do not know, but I am unwilling to stop. I must go on."

John Wesley Powell
(Grand Canyon expedition of 1869)

THE DIRT ROADS WERE not well maintained but were heavily traveled. In summer, the air was thick with the dust thrown up by the hoofs of the oxen and the churning wheels of the wagons. Relief came occasionally when a slight breeze came, but a strong wind only made things worse. Winter brought slower progress. If the roads were not frozen with ice and snow, they were deep in mud. There would be the occasional tavern or inn along the way where a weary traveler could get a meal and find a place to sleep, but most nights were spent on the hard planks of a covered wagon or on the ground under a starry sky. After passing St Louis, Missouri there would be no inns and taverns to speak of. You were very much on your own. During the summer, on a good day, one could travel twenty miles. In winter, five miles would be pushing it. In 1868, a person leaving Elmira, New York traveling west to homestead in southern Idaho could expect the rugged and demanding journey to take four months and cost between $400 and $1,500. In 1869, with the completion of the transcontinental railroad, the same trip would be cut to just seven days and cost as little as $70. Seventy-five years later, not much had changed as a young twenty-one-year-old farm girl from a little town south of Sun Valley, Idaho, Lois Manwill, worked her way east along the same route with only a single suitcase.

When Lois stepped off the train in Elmira, New York in February 1943, she was met by a tall, strapping young man from Utah who introduced himself as John Larsen. This first encounter produced two opposite reactions: he was smitten, she was not. After John left the train station that morning, he confided in a close friend that he had just met the girl he would one day marry. The young farm girl always kept a very detailed journal, and her entry on that same day briefly described having met a young man from Utah, but that was all she wrote. She recorded no other thoughts. Apparently, she was not overly impressed. When John returned from New York to Salt Lake City, the country was at war in the most horrific conflict in history, World War II. John had a deep and abiding love for his country, so instead of waiting to be drafted, he enlisted. He served in the Pacific from September 1943 to March 1946. Most of his time was aboard the USS Cambria as an Rm 3/c petty officer. During the war, he continued to correspond with Lois, and when he came home on leave for two weeks in September of 1945, he invited Lois to travel from Richfield, Idaho to Salt Lake City, Utah to meet his family. Following a nice lunch, John took Lois into the living room, sat her down on the couch and slipped a ring onto her finger. Her journal entry on that day reads, "John gave me a ring today and asked me to marry him. I have no idea why. Obviously, he has feelings for me that I definitely don't have for him." When I came across that entry, I thought, "How in the world did these two ever make it?" John refused to give up and continued to court her through letters for the remainder of the war. The total number of letters written by John to Lois during the war was 252. As World War II came to a close, John came to the conclusion that maybe he wasn't going to win fair maiden after all, so he wrote a letter to Lois, which included the following: "Lois, maybe this courtship isn't going to work after all, so why don't you just send the ring back and we will just be friends." That letter was a wakeup call to her. The thought of no longer having him in her life was very disconcerting. She suddenly realized that maybe she did have feelings for him after all. He returned from the war on February 5, 1946, and they were married April 6 of that same year. I was born six years later.

I always believed that Dad's "Faint heart never won fair maiden" applied to dating and courtship. But over time, I have realized it applies to any worthy endeavor in life. He always asked, "Is your heart really in it? Do you really believe?"

The poster read: "Come and join 180 high school students from across the Wasatch front in six glorious, fun-filled weeks in Europe. College credit will be given as we will learn about the culture, history, traditions, and art of five beautiful countries. We will be visiting such places as the Eiffel Tower, the Louvre and the Palace of Versailles in France, the Vatican, Venice, and Pompeii in Italy, the Bavarian Alps in Germany, Big Ben, Westminster Abbey, and Windsor Castle in England, and so much more. The tour includes food, lodging, air fare, and all entrance fees to the places we will visit."

The advertising poster hung in the front hallway of our school. The company behind the tour was the Foreign Study Language League. My assistant high school principal encouraged me to go on this trip whenever he saw me, but my response was always the same: "Dr. Burton, I would love to go, but there is no way my family could afford to send me." And his response was also always the same: "Brent, the company is offering one scholarship to a deserving student that covers all expenses, so why don't you apply?" And again, my response was the same: "Dr. Burton, my grades are far from stellar. They're even far below average, so it would be a waste of time to apply." After about the fifth such conversation, I realized that Dr. Burton was a very persistent man and that there was only one way to end this repetitive discussion, and so I finally applied. Three months before the tour was to leave, I received a letter from the company notifying me that I had been awarded the scholarship. I immediately thought that it was a scam, and so I contacted the company to ask two questions. The first question was, "How many of these scholarship award notices were sent out?" Their response was, "Just one, and it was sent to you." My second question was, "Why in the world was I awarded the scholarship?" their answer was simple: "Because you were the only one that applied." So, in the summer of 1969, I spent six magical weeks in Europe with 179 other high school students. I have often reflected on this experience, and I have come to a simple realization: if you don't try, you already know the outcome. As the great hockey player Wayne Gretzky once said, "You will miss 100% of the shots you don't take."

Historical

John Wesley Powell, Intrepid Grand Canyon and Colorado River Explorer

My oldest son once said that if he ever had a mistress, it would be the Grand Canyon.

To stand on the rim looking down into the Grand Canyon is breathtaking, but to stand in the bottom of the canyon looking up is life changing. The majesty is beyond description. Kevin Fedarko in his book *The Emerald Mile* comes close. "On any given evening in summer, but most notably in late June. There comes a moment just after the sun has disappeared behind the rimrock, and just before the darkness has tumbled down the walls, when the bottom of the Grand Canyon gives itself over to a moment muted grace that feels something like an act of Atonement for the sins of the world. This is the fleeting interregnum between the blast-furnace heat of the day and the star-draped immensity of the night, and when it arrives, the bedrock bathes in a special kind of light, the pink-and-orange blush of a freshly opened nectarine. This is also the canyon's loveliest hour. When there is nothing sweeter, nothing more calming to the soul, than standing along the shallows at the edge of the Colorado River and breathing in the wonders of that place."

John Wesley Powell was a thirty-five-year-old major, standing five foot six and weighing only 125 pounds. His father was a Methodist preacher in Wisconsin where John grew up. In 1861, as a lieutenant serving under Ulysses S. Grant at the Battle of Shiloh in southwestern Tennessee, he lost his right arm from a Confederate Minnie ball. He continued to serve in the Union Army until January 1865, reaching the rank of major. Two years later, he found himself as a natural history and geology professor at Illinois State University and working at the Illinois State Natural History Society. While collecting specimens for the museum, he hit upon the idea of exploring the mighty Colorado River for scientific purposes.

The year was 1869, and the setting was Green River, Wyoming, a small frontier town on the banks of the river that carried the same name. The population of this small community was just over 2,000. It was pretty much a forgotten town. If it was not for the mighty river that flowed throughout the center of town, it would probably not exist at all. It was here that Major John Wesley Powell assembled his ragtag crew of nine men, most of whom had little or no experience in boating, and some could not even swim.

The men had no way of knowing what to expect. The river could slowly descend or drop off in a major waterfall. They only knew that from their beginning point at Green River Station and their anticipated endpoint, the river would drop some 5,280 feet. None of these men had ever experienced white water or rapids of any kind.

Three of the boats they were to take, weighed close to half a ton each. They were twenty-one feet in length and had the capacity to carry approximately 2,000 pounds of cargo. All four boats were ill-suited for river running. They were hard to control because they had been designed for the calm waters of lakes and harbors.

They were to face some 500 rapids before their journey ended. Most rapids in the United States are ranked on a scale of one to five, yet because of the mighty diversity and complexity of the Colorado River, the ranking is one to ten, one is a rather mild and a delightful ride, and a ten is equal to some of the great rapids in the country. People can die in such rapids if they're not careful.

By August 10, Powell and his men had reached the Little Colorado, a small tributary that entered the main Colorado on their left. To them, it was nothing more than a muddy little stream, but when the water runs clear, this "little stream" transforms itself into one of the most vibrant turquoise colors that Mother Nature could ever create. The confluence of these two rivers is sacred to the Hopi Indian Tribe.

From his own diary, we gain an incredible insight that John Wesley Powell, of all men, had anything but a faint heart.

"We are now ready to start on our way down the great unknown. We are three-quarters of a mile in the depths of the earth, and the great river shrinks into insignificance, as it dashes its angry waves against the walls and cliffs that rise to the world above. They are but puny ripples, and we are but pygmies, running up and down the sand, or lost among the boulders. We have an unknown distance yet to run; an unknown river yet to explore. What falls there are, we know not; what rocks beset the channel, we know not; what walls rise over the river, we know not. What lies ahead I do not know, but I am unwilling to stop. I must go on."

By the end of their incredible journey, the men of the expedition had nothing left to give.

> "The men were unshaven, sunburned, their clothes threadbare, almost nonexistent, and all nearing starvation. The only supplies they had left were a day's rationing of flour and a small amount of coffee beans. On the bow of the lead boat was a small, tattered piece of cloth, what was left of the Stars and Stripes."
>
> *The Emerald Mile*

Ninety-nine days after leaving Green River Station and having traveled over 1,000 miles down an unknown and treacherous river, Powell and his men would end their expedition near the Grand Wash Cliffs where the Colorado enters present day Lake Mead.

CHAPTER 2

"UNTIL MY DOINGS CATCH UP WITH MY KNOWINGS, I AIN'T GOT TIME FOR NEW LEARNIN'S"

Education /
Learning

"We choose to go to the moon, we choose to go to the moon in this decade, and do the other things, not because they are easy, but because they are hard."

President John F. Kennedy

YEARS LATER IN REMINISCING about his college days, Dad wrote, "I suppose as a freshman and sophomore that I wasn't going to let my formal studies stand in the way of my education. All of those warm, sunny afternoons on the beach of the Great Salt Lake did not compensate for Ds in bacteriology and chemistry. With medical school out of the picture, I went to help Dad on the farm." It was definitely true that he really didn't have time for "new learnin's."

His time on the farm, then living in New York, followed by two and a half years in the South Pacific during World War II gave John plenty of opportunities to contemplate what it was he really wanted out of life. During that time, he came to an epiphany that would change his life: *knowledge is power.* Power to build, to grow, to motivate others, to achieve your life's dreams, and to control your own destiny. From the time he returned from World War II in April 1946 until his death a little over fifty years later, he embarked on a journey of learning and discovery that never ceased.

I rarely saw Dad without a book either in his hand or nearby. He was a voracious reader and his thirst for knowledge was never quenched. His personal library consisted of over 10,000 volumes. He instilled in me a great love for the arts, native cultures, science, and especially history. Whenever we traveled as a family and came across a roadside historical marker, a museum or a site on the National Register of Historic Places, we knew instinctively that Dad was going to stop. We seldom minded. Dad had an amazing gift. He could describe some historical events in such a way that we felt we had actually traveled back in time to witness the event firsthand. We were there at the driving of the golden spike where the Union and Central Pacific railroads first met in northern Utah on May 10, 1869, completing the transcontinental railroad. We witnessed the signing of the Declaration of Independence on July 2, 1776, the day that the continental congress voted for independence. We felt the concussions of the bombs from the Japanese torpedo bombers as they tore through the deck of the USS Arizona on December 7, 1941, at Pearl Harbor. We experienced the wind on our face, blowing in from the sea at Kill Devil Hills, North Carolina as we witnessed the first powered flight in history, watching Wilbur Wright take to the air for eleven seconds on December 17, 1903. Dad also introduced us to many great authors. Men and women who had the creative ability to bring amazing people to life. One of these authors was David McCullough. When Dad suggested that I read his book on Harry S. Truman, *Truman*, I was discouraged by its sheer volume My attention span is relatively short, and so the 1,117 pages of *Truman* kept me from even attempting the read. Dad even gave me his copy of the book as a gift, still to no avail. The book simply went on the shelf and there it remained for the next ten years. It wasn't until after Dad had passed away that I came across the book, and I contemplated on why he had been so high on it. I assumed it was because Truman had been the President of the United States when he was younger and raising a family of his own, and therefore the book *Truman* was more relevant to him. So, I started to read the book more out of a curiosity to find out why Dad had enjoyed it so much. I was a young boy when Harry Truman was still alive, but I knew little of his personal and political life, and so I decided to jump in. I soon found myself unable to set the book down. The more I learned about Truman, the more I came to understand why Dad had been encouraging me to read the book. When my wife and I traveled through Independence, Missouri a few years later, I had to stop at the home where Truman had lived, and we also visited the Truman Presidential Library. One of the displays in the library showed two surveys taken of college professors from across the country. Their expertise was in the fields of history and political science. The first survey was conducted just after Truman left office, and the other one was compiled fifty years later. The first survey taken when he left the White House rated him as one of the five worst presidents ever to hold office, and the other more recent survey ranked him as one of the top five presidents to ever serve. His accomplishments included his "Fair Deal," which expanded public housing, increased aid to public education, and instituted a higher minimum wage and federal protection for civil rights. Other accomplishments included desegregating the military, recognizing the creation of Israel, and expanding social security, He also instituted the Truman Doctrine and the Marshall Plan to help rebuild Europe after the terrible destruction caused by World War II. He accomplished so much, especially for a farm boy from Missouri who never had a college degree and never owned his own home. His motto, which was on a plaque on his desk, read simply, "The Buck Stops Here." I soon found myself reading McCullough's other books: *John Adams*, *1776*, *Brooklyn Bridge* and *Pathway to the Sea*. In fact, I have read almost every book he has written, and I have enjoyed them all. There are so many good historical writers: David McCullough, Stephen Ambrose, Doris Kearns Goodwin, Ron Chernow, Walter Isaacson, Candice Millard, Edmund Morris, and many others. Another odyssey Dad has sent me on is to learn more about the young president Teddy Roosevelt. He was at the top of Dad's list of great leaders, and I wanted to know why Dad felt the way he had about thirty-sixth president, and so I started to read book after book about the man: *The Rise of Theodore Roosevelt*, *Theodore Rex*, *The River of Doubt*, *Mornings on Horseback*, and others. I was thoroughly captivated by the man, and his bigger than life personality. I have one major regret, and that is that I had not learned more about Teddy Roosevelt earlier in my life. I could have spent hours discussing him with Dad. He would have given me such rich insights. I regret the opportunity lost. He who hesitates loses.

As far as my early education was concerned, I found myself following in my father's early footsteps. I couldn't let my education get in the way of my learning either. But the difference between the two of us was that dad managed to change when he was twenty-four years old. As for me, well, I'm still a work in progress.

Historical

Apollo Moon Landing — One of the most incredible achievements in human history

The first American in space was Alan Shepard. His flight lasted only fifteen minutes, and it occurred on May 5, 1961. Twenty days later, President John F. Kennedy addressed Congress about urgent national needs and said, "This nation should commit itself to achieve the goal, before the decade is out, of landing a man on the moon." Sixteen months later, he gave his profound speech concerning space exploration while addressing the students and faculty at Rice University.

"We set sail on this new sea because there is new knowledge to be gained and new rights to be won, and they must be won and used for the progress of all people.

"We choose to go to the moon, we choose to go to the moon in this decade and do the other things, not because they are easy, but because they are hard. Because the goal will serve to organize and measure the best of our energies and skills. Because the challenge is one we are willing to accept, one we are unwilling to postpone, and one which we intend to win. Even though I realize that this is in some measure an act of faith and vision, for we do not know what benefits await us. But if I were to say, my fellow citizens, that we shall send to the moon 240,000 miles away from the control station in Houston, a giant rocket more than 300 feet tall, the length of a football field, made of new metal alloys, some of which have not yet been invented, capable of a precision better than the finest watch, carrying all the equipment needed for propulsion, guidance, control, communication, food and survival, on an untried mission, to an unknown celestial body, and then return it safely to the earth, re-entering the atmosphere at speeds of over 25,000 miles per hour, causing heat about half that of the temperature of the sun, and do all this, and do it right, and do it before this decade is out, then we must be bold."

Address given at Rice University
September 12, 1962

It is hard to believe that from the time this speech was delivered on September 12, 1962, until the realization of this incredible dream with Neil Armstrong setting foot on the moon on July 20, 1969, it was only six years, ten months and nine days. A feat unequaled in the history of the world.

The device that would ultimately carry Neil Armstrong and Buzz Aldrin to the surface of the moon would be the largest and most complex engine ever made: the Saturn V Rocket. In 1998, I visited the Kennedy Space Center in Florida. As I stood under this magnificent engine, I felt dwarfed by its massive size and technical design.

Some of the amazing statistics and daunting challenges required to put a man on the moon are listed below.

The number of people who worked on the Apollo program was 400,000, with an average age of twenty-six years old.

Saturn V Rocket

- The first to use the rocket was the crew of Apollo 8.
- The rocket was capable of sending men to the surface of the moon 238,855 miles away with speeds from 15,647 miles an hour up to 25,000 to escape earth's orbit.
- It was 363 ft high (36 stories) 33 feet in diameter and weighed 6.5 million pounds at liftoff.

Propellant

- The fuel used in only the first second was ten times more than the fuel used by Charles Lindberg in his historic 3,600-mile flight from New York to Paris in 1927.
- The first stage burned twenty tons of fuel per second.
- It burned 4.5 million pounds of fuel in the first two minutes and forty-one seconds, with thrust equivalent to 160 million HP or 7.6 million pounds of thrust (equivalent to the power generated by eighty-five Hoover Dams).
- The total fuel used was 4,700,000 pounds.
- Eighty-nine railroad cars of liquid oxygen and twenty-eight cars of liquid hydrogen with twenty-seven of kerosene were used.

Capsule

- The capsule contained a command module with life support systems.
- The capsule that carried the Apollo 11 crew was built with over two million individual parts, fifteen miles of wire, a control panel with twenty-four instruments, 566 switches, forty indicators, and seventy-one lights.
- The round trip was over 500,000 miles.

Computers

- MIT developed the computers used. At the time when computers were huge and were running on punch cards. The ones needed for the capsule would be bigger than the space capsule itself. MIT was able to design a small computer the size of a briefcase using integrated circuits and computer chips.

Spacesuit

- The spacesuit is capable of sustaining life independently against the most hostile environment known to man. A small cut in the suit could cause the blood to actually boil. It had to protect against temperatures of over 250 degrees Fahrenheit in the sunlight and a minus 250 degrees Fahrenheit in the shade.

  The spacesuit also incorporated:

  Twenty-one layers of nested fabric

  Pressure-tight helmet

  Gold-coated sun visor

  Backpack with communication radio

  Oxygen

  Dehumidifier

  Pressure gauge

  Circulating fan

  Emergency container

  Emergency oxygen system

  Communication radio

  Microphone

  Antenna

  Backpack remote control unit

  Urine collection system

  Emergency self-sealing patch for medication

  Coolant water pump

  Liquid-cooled underwear

  Lunar overshoes with tractor-tread soles

  Protective gloves

Heat Shield to Re-enter Earth's Atmosphere

- The space capsule would be traveling 25,000 miles per hour, creating heat from friction of 5,000 degrees Fahrenheit, which is hot enough to vaporize metal.

- Avco, a company out of Massachusetts, created a solution. They developed a heat-resistant resin, with a honeycomb framework that was used to hold the resin in place with 370,000 cells. Each cell had to be filled by hand, one cell at a time, with the newly developed resin.

Lunar Module (LEM)

- The LEM was so fragile that a grain of sand could puncture its skin.

- It was a two-stage vehicle to take the astronauts from the command module to the surface of the Moon and return them back again.

- It was covered with an extremely thin metal skin and required no aerodynamic design because it was operating in the vacuum of space and weighed 8,600 pounds,

Parachutes Used During Reentry

- Three were used, with each measuring 83.5 feet across (7,200 square feet of fabric, 3.5 miles of thread and two million stitches)

- Only three people in the entire country were authorized by the FAA to pack the chutes, and their job was considered so critical that they were never allowed to travel together so the program would not lose them all if there was an accident.

Final Thought

How far we have come in just a mere sixty-six years. From a small wooden framed plane with muslin covered wings traveling 120 feet at thirty miles an hour at Kill Devil Hills, North Carolina on December 17, 1903, to the Saturn V Rocket traveling a total of 953,054 miles, at speeds of up to 25,000 miles per hour carrying the first men to the Sea of Tranquility on the surface of the Moon on July 21, 1969. It is significant that Neil Armstrong took with him to the surface of the Moon aboard the lunar module *Eagle* a plaque containing an 8-by-13 piece of muslin fabric from the left wing of the Wright Brothers' 1903 *Flyer*.

The Apollo program cost $25 billion. The American flag left behind by astronauts Neil Armstrong and Buzz Aldrin cost $5.50.

CHAPTER 3

"BE A MEMBER OF THE CONSTRUCTION CREW, AND NOT A MEMBER OF THE WRECKING GANG"

Positive influence / Making a difference

"Far better it is to dare mighty things, to win glorious triumphs even though checkered by failure, than to rank with those poor spirts who neither enjoy nor suffer much because they live in the gray twilight that knows not victory nor defeat."

Teddy Roosevelt

THERE ARE TWO KINDS of people in the world: those who create problems and those who solve them. So, if you don't like the way things are working out, don't complain unless you have a suggestion or plan to make it better, and then become a force for good in making that change.

Dad was often quoting poets, presidents, world leaders, religious giants, etc. One person he always admired was

Teddy Roosevelt, who was president of the United States from September 1901 to March 1909. After leaving the presidency, Teddy undertook an extended world tour with his second son, Kermit, and after spending ten months in Africa, he was joined by his wife, Edith, to tour Europe. Everywhere he went, he was met with massive crowds, many anxious to simply get a glimpse of the man who just the previous year had been the most powerful man on earth, and definitely the most colorful. One of Dad's oft-quoted Roosevelt gems was from a speech Roosevelt delivered at the Sorbonne, in Paris France on April 23, 1910. The speech was entitled "Citizens in a Republic." The quote has often been labeled "The Man in The Arena."

"It's not the critic who counts. Not the man who points out how the strong man stumbles, or where the doer of deeds could have done them better. The credit belongs to the man who is actually in the arena, whose face is marred by dust and sweat and blood; who strives valiantly; who errs; who comes short again and again, because there is no effort without error and shortcomings — but who does actually strive to do the deeds; who knows great enthusiasms, the great devotions; who spends himself in a worthy cause; who, at the best, knows in the end the triumph of high achievement, and who, at the worst, if he fails, at least fails while daring greatly, so that his place shall never be with those cold and timid souls who neither know victory nor defeat."

"Be a member of the construction crew," Dad would always say. "Always leave a place or a person better than when you found them. Fix up, lift up, and cheer up, everything and everyone you come in contact with. The world should be a better place because you were there."

Being a member of the construction crew probably was reinforced from Dad's experiences in World War II. The Axis powers, consisting of Hitler's Germany, Mussolini's Italy, and Emperor Hirohito's Japan, combined to create the greatest "wrecking gang" in the history of the world. Their influence would negatively affect the lives of every single person on earth, with the death of over seventy million people, the leveling of entire cities and the near annihilation of entire cultures. The Allied forces made up of the U.S., England, France, Russia, and the rest of the world, combined to create the "construction crew." Their collective desire was to build for the world a better tomorrow. It was a mission founded in the belief that hope, peace, and prosperity would eventually rule supreme.

Historical

Dad's journal entries from WW II in the Pacific Theater

Dad was part of what Tom Brokaw called "The Greatest Generation." He wrote a book by the same name about the young men and women who fought in World War II.

My favorite holiday has always been the Fourth of July. That seed was planted early in life with Dad. He had a deep and abiding love for his country. In World War II, because Dad was working on a farm, he qualified for a deferment. Many jobs were considered vital for the support of the war effort, and food production was considered essential. Instead, he chose to leave the farm and to enlist. He sailed to Hawaii aboard the aircraft carrier *Saratoga*. There he was trained as a radio operator. He served in the Pacific from September 14, 1943 to March 26,1946. He was assigned to the *USS Cambria,* which at one point became the flagship for Admiral Hill. He was going aboard as an Rm 3/c petty officer. Life aboard ship was fairly uneventful and routine, but on shore in a foxhole, that quickly changed. I remember his description of the food they ate, called "K-rations. Dad said "the first few days when you opened a can and found weevil (a very small beetle) in the food, you would throw the whole thing away. After a few days of going hungry you would pick out the weevil and eat the food. After a few more days, you would pick out the food, throw it away, and eat the weevil.

He was in five major campaigns in the Pacific Theater. All of the following accounts of these battles have come from his personal journals.

Saipan was his first.

"For four hours prior to dawn, an air cover softened up the beaches and then the Marines started over the side and onto the beach. Thousands were killed within minutes. For these invasions, they sent in a communications team with the first wave of fighters. They were to establish a beachhead and set up a ship to shore communications to direct the landing of the rest of the troops. The members of the beach party from our ship were wiped out the first day and the next morning at muster, our division officer asked if there were any volunteers that would make up a new communications team for a new beach party, Russ Berg and I immediately stepped forward and volunteered. We really didn't know what we were volunteering for at the time — just a new adventure, I guess. Anything to help get this war over and get back home. I'm sure there were a lot of relieved men from our division when we volunteered, for no one else ever stepped forward. Within hours we were outfitted with proper fighting gear, radios, and guns, and were on our way onto Red Beach. We got there, dug a foxhole, and set up our radio just in time for a counterattack by the Japanese. When dawn broke the following day, we noticed a piece of shrapnel about eighteen inches long, triangular in shape and about five inches on each side — very jagged and sharp laying right in the foxhole with us just inches from where we were lying. If it had hit us, it would have torn us to bits. For the next four days we didn't get any real sleep as we directed the landing of troops and supplies. On the third night, a small boat approached the beach with an officer aboard who didn't realize the password had changed. (Passwords were used especially at night to identify each other as being friend or foe.) In giving an old password, someone opened fire on them. The string of cuss words that filed the air soon let us know that it wasn't the enemy. No self-respecting Japanese would have known those words, and if he had, he would never have used them. At any rate, the cussing kept him alive, and he was able to land. As the troops moved inland, we followed along, moving into what had been the town of Sharon Kanoe. All that was left was a wall of a building here and there. The fighting on the island was fierce and the Japanese moved toward the north end with a high cliff where they jumped to their death rather than being taken prisoner. The taking of Saipan was critical to the pacific campaign. It became the air base for B 29s and placed them within striking distance of mainland Japan. Plans were then made for the invasion of Tinian."

Tinian was next.

"Tinian was a small island that was used as an officers training center for the Japanese military. Again, the following is from Dad's journal:

"The morning of the invasion was a stormy, rainy day. The wind was blowing hard and the channel between the two islands was very rough. The invasion plan was for all troops to embark from Saipan and cross the channel in LSDs (Landing Ship Dock), about fifty men per boat. Once again, our communications team was selected to go in with the first wave and set up communications to direct the landing of the rest of the troops. I never remember ever being at sea in any rougher water than that. It was so rough that even the coxswain, who drove the landing craft and spent most of his in choppy water, got seasick. It was a chain reaction from one man to the next, right down the side of the landing craft. We got ashore without any of our group being wounded, but by the time we landed we were all so sick and weak that the enemy could have knocked us all down with fly swatters. The island had many large caves all around a high plateau in the center of the island. Each of these caves had large cannons in them all pointing out to sea to discourage any invading forces. These caves were so well-reinforced with cement and steel that our bombing planes had not made a dent during the softening-up process the three days prior to the invasion. Great steel and cement doors were at the entrance of each cave."

Years later, reflecting back on the invasion, Dad commented,

"I wonder how we ever took the island from the Japanese. I suppose the inexperience of the Japanese forces garrisoned there was in our favor. The stakes were high."

After Tinian, a call came for a radio landing team for a new invasion, there were several teams who volunteered so a coin was flipped to see who would go first, and dad's team lost. At the time Dad was very disappointed but soon realized the hand of providence. Every member of the first team lost their lives in the first wave. The battle was Iwo Jima.

Following a little downtime on the big Island of Hawaii, preparations were made for the next campaign, and dad soon found himself headed for the first invasion of the Philippines. This took place at Lingayen Gulf, as recorded by Dad.

"The night before the invasion, no one slept. There was excitement in getting ready to go ashore. They always cooked us a big steak dinner at about 4:00 a.m. It was kind of a 'last gesture before the end' type of thing. Our navy always set up some kind of diversionary tactic for each invasion. A group of ships and planes hammered an area for three days before the invasion in hopes the enemy would divert all of their troops to that area in anticipation of an attempted landing at that point. Then the real attack force would sneak in at another point, shell it very hard for three or four hours and then send the troops in. This was just partially successful in Lingayen. At 7:00 a.m. we were in landing crafts forming up just off the ships, and then we set off for the beach with shells screaming overhead from both directions. It was interesting how the day started off with a brilliant red sun coming up out of the ocean like an omen of the kind of day it would be. We hit the beach and very quickly dug in and had our ship to shore radio set up to give directions for the landing of the main strike force. The Japanese were determined to keep us from establishing a beachhead, and we were just as determined to push ahead. By evening we had pushed in about 500 yards. It was so precarious that first night that we changed the password every three hours. If you moved around very much, you had better remember the new password, because if you were challenged and your response with the correct password was not given quickly enough, you didn't get a second chance to give it."

This section is about Leyte in the Philippines, where the fighting continued.

"We were dug in on the beach and had things going pretty well with the landing of all the reserve troops when the first of two incidents occurred. It was during a retaliatory bombing mission that the Japanese made on our particular beach. We were scrunched down in our foxhole as deep as we could get and we could hear the planes coming in, dropping their bombs. I could hear them explode with a thunderous and louder whump, whump, whump, getting closer with each explosion. When they finished their round and we came out, we could see this row of big holes going along in a line to within twenty feet of our foxhole, and I was not hurt. The next day, a group of suicide Kamikaze planes flew in and were strafing the beach. When these planes came in, I think it was one of the times I knew real fear. I could hear those machine gun bullets zinging all around me. By the time they had finished and crashed their planes, I got up -and looked around me and, in a two-by-six-inch plank that had just been in front of my face, was a chunk of lead that did not find its mark. When I got back to my foxhole, my buddy K. Burg was sitting there crying and telling me how lucky I was, because a Marine coming up the beach when the strafing started had jumped into my foxhole for protection, and while in there, one of the bullets from the Japanese plane hit and killed him. I, too, sat down and wept. That could have easily been me. After securing Leyte, we headed for Manila. I was part of the initial landing to direct the landing troops. By the time we got to the city proper, the enemy was totally subdued there. The city had been so demolished from the softening-up process that there wasn't a building left standing. I had never seen such destruction up to this time."

Okinawa was his final engagement.
This was one of the bloodiest battles of the entire war. It is estimated that there were over 49,000 American casualties, including about 12,000 deaths. About 90,000 Japanese combatants died in the

fighting and death among the civilians may have been as high as 150,000.

Dad was there only three days before his ship was hit and ordered back to the states for repairs. So, his journal has very few entries.

On August 6, 1945, President Harry S. Truman ordered a single B-29 to drop the first atomic bomb on Hiroshima, leveling 4.4 square miles of the city and killing between seventy and eighty thousand people. Three days later on August 9, Nagasaki was bombed.

After the destruction of Hiroshima, Admiral Hill was aboard the *USS Cambria* and was ordered to accept surrender for that part of the empire. The main surrender where the articles of surrender were signed by the Japanese Imperial Staff took place aboard the *USS Missouri* with General Douglas MacArthur in Tokyo Bay on August 10, 1945. Dad again recorded his experience.

"After the ceremonies, we moved into the bay and I shall never forget as long as I live that scene: the twisted masses of steel, the destroyed shipyards, the burned hills, the floating, bloated dead bodies, the people with one side of their body scabbed with scars and oozing sores as the result of the atomic blast. To look out over the flat area where the main part of the city had once stood, there was not a single building left standing: not a tree or a shrub, nothing but rubble and desolation. It was far more than anyone could ever envision.

When Admiral Hill was ready to make his inspection of the area, he wanted a radio operator to be part of his company, and I was selected to be that operator. Anytime he went anyplace, I went along in the Admiral's gig. On one visit, we went to a submarine construction dock and what we saw gave us cause to rejoice that the Japanese had surrendered. They were building hundreds of little one-man operated submarines which would have been transported close to the American shore and launched. They would have moved in close and fired their torpedoes, all of which was part of a suicide mission. I climbed down in one of them and wondered how anyone could ever psych themselves up to be part of any such operation when confined in such small quarters. The navigator would have to be in a lying-down position all the time that he was aboard."

With the war over, the government established a point system so that military personnel could be discharged in an orderly way. It was based on the number of years and months of service and the major battles one had been in. Dad had enough points to be immediately discharged, but someone had to bring the servicemen home, and his ship was assigned to what became known as "Magic Carpet Duty." As a result, his assignment on board the ship would continue.

One of these trips took Dad to Tokyo and Yokohama, bringing men back to Seattle. Another was from Shanghai to San Francisco. One day while in Shanghai, he recorded this tender experience:

"A young boy had attached himself to us this day because I had given him something from my K-ration pack. He followed us until it was nearly time for us to go back to our ship and he realized that he couldn't go with us any longer. He gathered up some newspapers, spread them on the ground in a doorway of a store where he would be a little bit sheltered and laid down on what was to be his bed for the night. It was bitter cold. It was one of those occasions where you wished you could smuggle him aboard ship and adopt him. He was a boy I would judge to be about eight years old."

Following three trips, the ship was needed in the Atlantic. After going throughout the Panama Canal and up to Newport, Virginia, Dad left Virginia and traveled by bus back to San Francisco and the discharge center. It was March 26, 1946.

Every time Dad saw the American flag pass by in a parade or raised on a flagpole, he would immediately put his hand over his heart and stand reverently, usually with a tear in his eye, because he saw firsthand the ultimate sacrifices that many he personally knew made so that we might enjoy the freedoms we have been blessed with today.

CHAPTER 4

"A LARSEN CAN DO ANYTHING"

Optimism

"It is not really necessary to look too far into the future, we see enough already to be certain it will be magnificent. Only let us hurry and open the roads."

Wilbur Wright

WE FOUGHT, WE ARGUED, we teased, we laughed, and we cried as siblings, especially when Mom and Dad were not home. But the one thing we never did whether they were home or not was to say, "I can't." We could say, "I don't want to" or "I don't need to," but we could never, ever say, "I can't." It was one of those unwritten tenets of the very foundation of the Larsen home. In its place we were taught to say, "A Larsen can do anything." It was so driven home to us that we actually started to believe it. This belief has been traced back at least three generations. When Dad enlisted in World War II, his father, my grandfather Rube Larsen, sent him off to war with the following directive that Dad recorded in his journal on September 25, 1943: "You can do anything you want to, son. If you don't know all the particulars, you can learn them, but don't be afraid to assert yourself. You can do anything.

You can be a leader and go as far as you want to go. You can do anything you put your mind to as long as it's not immoral or illegal."

Dad was right. We are limited in our accomplishments in this life only by our own self-doubts, timidity, and lack of confidence.

This attitude has now been carried to the fourth generation. My youngest son Eric decided at age five that he wanted a new bike, and not just any bike. It had to be a specific bike — one he had found advertised in the local newspaper. It was a red ten speed with white racing stripes, and it was being sold at a local Kmart store and would cost $186.00. Eric approached me to see if I would buy it for him. I decided to make this a learning experience, so I made a deal with him. It was simple: if he would earn half the money, I would pitch in the other half. He was excited for the opportunity, and so was I because I knew it would be quite some time before a five-year-old could earn ninety-three dollars (his half of the money). I knew I would be safe for quite some time. I could not have been more wrong. The first thing Eric did was to approach his mother and say, "Mom, can I borrow fifty dollars?" She had heard of the agreement the two of us had made and reminded him that he was to earn his half of the money for the bike. He promised that he was only asking to borrow the money, and that he would soon pay her back. So, reluctantly, she loaned him the money. He then approached his older sister Liz and asked her if she would drive him to the nearest wholesale grocery store where he bought fifty dollars' worth of bulk candy, whistle pops, candy bars, and gum. Then, upon returning home, he took a small red wagon and built a wooden box on top. It was really quite clever. The cover on top of his box folded out so that he could put his candy on top as it created a display shelf for his wares. He then started going door to door selling his candy. At this point I was a little concerned at his tenacity, but ninety-three dollars was still a lot of money for a five-year-old to earn, and I knew his attention span would soon wane. At the end of the first day when he returned home, I asked him how it had gone, to which he replied, "Oh, not so great, I only sold six dollars' worth." Not bad for a little guy, but still a long way from his goal. The next day he came up with an idea that would prove to be a game changer. At the end of his second day, he had sold only a few more candy bars but was not discouraged in the least. When I asked him again how his second day had gone, he said, "Dad, I decided I could sell a lot more candy if I went to where there were more people to sell them to. So, I went down to the bottom of the hill where the school busses let the kids off after school." I asked, "So, how did you do?" He responded, "Not so good. None of the kids had any money, but I told them I would be there again tomorrow. So, if they brought money from home, I would have the candy ready for them. "

The kid hit a gold mine. Two buses with sixty kids each and twenty cents profit on each candy bar in a short fifteen-minute period. Well, you do the math. He also continued to work the neighborhood, not content with just the bus stop. I noticed after several days that there was one of the older kids shadowing Eric around after school. Josh was twelve years old and had quite a reputation as a bully, and I was concerned that he might be trying to steal Eric's money and candy. So, I asked Eric if Josh was giving him a hard time. He quickly responded, "Oh no, Dad. He's not trying to steal from me. He's protecting me. I hired him to be my bodyguard."

"What do you mean he's your bodyguard"? I asked.

"Oh, I was worried that someone might try to take my stuff, so I hired the meanest kid I know to protect me."

"And what do you pay Josh for his services?" I inquired.

"Oh," said Eric. "I give him twenty-five cents an hour and a free candy bar."

"Smart idea, son," I said as I walked away in disbelief of what a five-year-old was doing. Well, as you can imagine, it was less than ten days before he had not only paid his mother back the seed money he had borrowed, but he had also earned the ninety-three dollars for the bike that was his half of the agreement. I was now in serious trouble, so I did the only thing I could think of: I went to Eric's mother and asked for a fifty-dollar loan, and then asked Liz, my oldest daughter, to take me to the store.

I have always tried to fashion my life after the example of my father. The one constant was that Dad always led by example. It wasn't what he said, it was what he did. So, in 1978, I decided to put Dad's saying to the ultimate test. I came to the realization that if the dream of having our own home was ever going to come to fruition, then we would have to build it ourselves. It was during my first year of teaching at a local junior high school. We had very little income and my wife Tineke (a Dutch name) was a stay-at-home mother taking care of our three little children Liz, BJ, and Anna. I didn't know the first thing about construction other than having barely passed shop class when I was thirteen years old. The shoeshine box I built for my school project really wasn't very good, as evidenced by the fact that my mother had to ask what it was. I ran into a contractor one day, Ross, who was the father of a close friend. As we were talking, I learned that Ross was developing a new subdivision, and when I expressed interest in buying a building lot, he agreed to hold one of the lots for me until I could secure the financing to buy it. I found it difficult to secure the funding, but I was not going to let a little thing like money get in the way. I came up with this idea: Why should I just borrow enough money to buy the lot? Why not borrow enough money to build a house as well? I was surprised that the bank was unwilling to loan me the money. Of course, I had never built a house before, but didn't that shoeshine box count for something in the way of construction experience? I was not to be deterred, so I went back to Ross for help.

I said, "Ross I want to build my own home on the lot you are holding for me."

"Fine," he said, "I didn't know you were a contractor."

"Oh, I'm not," I replied.

"Well then. how do you suppose you are going to do it then?" he asked.

"Well, I am a fast learner and a hard worker," I said.

"That's fine," he said. "But no bank is going to loan you money based on desire alone."

"I know. I just found that out, and that's why I have come to see you. I would like to propose the following: if you would be willing, as a contractor, to sign a letter to the bank guaranteeing the completion of the house, then, I think, with that guarantee behind the project, the bank might be willing to go for it. And to make it worth your risk in doing this for me, I will pay you a fee. And if I am unable to finish the house, I will give you everything I have put into it, both labor and materials."

When he hesitated, I pulled out my trump card. "Ross, if I was your son, what would you tell me to do?"

Ross replied, "I would tell you to go for it."

And so, the letter was sent, and the loan was made. The amount of money we had to work with was very tight, even by 1978 standards. The loan was for only $41,000. This was all the money we had to not only buy the lot but also build the house. This created the necessity to do everything we could possibly do ourselves and at the same time complete the house in under six months, because the interest we were paying was high enough that if we went past that time frame, the financing would become almost impossible.

As I got started, I soon realized that I might have underestimated the difficulty of the task ahead. But I kept telling myself, "Remember, a Larsen can do anything." After getting the footings and foundation in (not without its challenges), it was time to start framing. I remember going down the hill to where another home was under construction to ask the builder, Jay, a few basic questions about framing so that I could get started. Questions like, "What do you call those boards that sit on top of the foundation that the flooring rests on (floor joists)? And what do you call those two-by-fours that you build the walls with (studs)? And how long do you cut them? And how far apart are they spaced (92 5/8 long, spaced sixteen inches on center)? And what does 'on center' mean?"

After several minutes, Jay asked me why I was asking all these questions. I replied, "Oh, I'm building my own house up the street and I needed to know how to get started." The look on Jay's face was one of disbelief, but I was not discouraged. "Remember," I thought, "I am a fast learner. I learned everything I could through reading books and observing other trades and sometimes just through dumb luck."

But eventually the house started to take shape. When it came time to do the electrical, I figured my wife Tineke could handle it, so I told her to go around to other construction sites, find one where there was an electrician's truck parked out in front, and then to go in and follow the man around asking questions about what he is doing and why. He will probably enjoy the company. So, the questions came: "What wire do you use? Where do you place the electrical boxes and how far apart? How do you wire a light?" Tineke would ask the questions, take copious notes, and then return to our house and duplicate the process. She even wired the main electrical breaker box. This had me a little worried, so I hired an electrician for one hour to come and inspect her work. He gave her two thumbs up. We also learned how to roof, set tiles, sheetrock, install exterior siding, hang doors and windows, paint, and do finish carpentry, among other trades. I recently drove by the old house and saw that after thirty-seven years, the house is still standing, even if the front hall light still burns only half bright.

We are the product of all of the accumulated experiences of past generations. What my grandfather learned, my father improved upon, and I was expected to perfect. It hasn't always played out that way, but the concept is noteworthy.

Historical

The Wright Brothers first powered flight—Ingenuity and perseverance that changed the world

July 20, 1969, started out just like any other ordinary day, but by nightfall the entire world was riveted to the television sets at home or in store front windows watching an event unfold that was the culmination of a dream mankind had held deep in its heart ever since man gazed into the heavens. The words heard around the world that day were these: "That's one small step for a man, one giant leap for mankind," We watched almost in disbelief as Neil Armstrong set foot on the moon, the first man to ever do so.

The ability to achieve this incredible feat started sixty-eight years earlier when a young man named Wilbur Wright sat at his workbench holding a square piece of cardboard and started to twist it one way and then the other. He realized that true sustained manned flight required more than just power, it required control, and from a piece of cardboard came the concept of "wing warping," or twisting the wing to gain lateral control, later called "roll control." Others had spent years designing aircraft. Alexander Graham Bell, who invented the telephone, felt that the ideal flying machine would be a kite affair built of equilateral triangles — a sort of tetrahedral cell. Samuel Langley, head of the Smithsonian Institute, spent years using the vast resources of the Smithsonian and over $70,000 developing an aerodrome catapulted from a barge on the Potomac River. But by 1901, they had all failed. By contrast, the Wright Brothers would spend less than $1,000 to achieve their dream of sustained flight.

Methodically, Orville and his younger brother Wilbur tested design after design, even building a wind tunnel to test their theories. Then, using design #12, the two brothers traveled to the outer banks of North Carolina, a place called Kitty Hawk on Kill Devil Hills. They had spent the last three previous years there experimenting with different designs. Then on Dec 17, 1903, Orville Wright climbed aboard a small flying machine made of ash spruce and muslin with a forty-foot wingspan powered by a small twelve horsepower engine that they had built themselves, because one that small with that kind of power did not exist. For twelve glorious seconds, they flew 120 feet. By the fourth flight of the day, with Wilbur now at the controls, the plane flew 852 feet and remained aloft for fifty-nine seconds. The world would never be the same. It had changed forever.

The challenges they faced would, to many, seem insurmountable, but not to this intrepid duo. They truly believed that a "Wright could do anything," just as I was taught to believe that a Larsen also could.

A Little Background on the brothers

The Wright brothers were never afraid to try something new. They were inventors, mechanics shop owners, newspapermen, designers and builders. Most importantly, they were trailblazers, becoming the first to design, build and then fly the first powered aircraft in the history of mankind.

Wilbur: "From the time we were little children, my brother Orville and myself lived together, played together and worked together, and in fact, thought together. "

The brothers were inseparable and complemented each other perfectly.

Orville: "I got more thrills out of flying before I had ever been in the air at all, while lying in bed thinking how exciting it would be to fly."

In 1899, the year the brothers showed serious interest in flight, Wilbur and Orville Wright were living at 7 Hawthorn Street in Dayton, Ohio. Wilbur was thirty-two and Orville was twenty-eight and both were single. Wilbur was more serious than his brother, studied nonstop and was very reflective, which others interpreted as aloof. Orville, on the other hand, had a little more hair and a well-groomed mustache and dressed in beautifully tailored suits. Orville hated the limelight and appeared quite shy in public. He was more optimistic and cheerful but could become moody when he became overwhelmed. He had a real gift when it came to design and mechanics. When Orville started his own printing company in 1889 while still in high school, he built his own printing press using an old headstone, some metal scraps and a spring from an old buggy.

In 1893, the two brothers started a bicycle company, the Wright Cycle Exchange, repairing and selling bikes. By 1895, they were manufacturing their own bicycle, the Van Cleve, which sold for about $65. The bicycle company they started would have a profound influence on their later success in flight.

In a letter Wilbur had sent to the Smithsonian Institution in 1899, he wrote: "Birds are the most perfectly trained gymnasts in the world and are well-fitted for their work. I believe that simple flight at least is possible to man, and that the experiment and investigations of a large number of independent workers will result in the accumulation of information and knowledge and skill, which will finally lead to accomplished flight. I have been interested in the problem of human and mechanical flight ever since as a boy I constructed a number of bats of various sizes. My observations since have only convinced me more firmly that human flight is possible and practical. It is only a question of knowledge and skill as in all acrobatic feats."

In his letter, he continued, "I have some pet theories as to the proper construction of a flying machine. I am about to begin a systematic study of the subject in preparation for practical work to which I expect to devote what time I can spare from my regular business. I wish to obtain such papers as the Smithsonian Institution has published on this subject, and if possible, a list of other works in print in English. I wish to avail myself of all that is already known and then, if possible, add my might to help the future worker who will attain final success."

Wilbur's letter could not have been sent at a more perfect time. When it came to scientific endeavors, the Smithsonian Institution was without question the most prestigious facility in the United States. In 1899, it was headed by Samuel Pierpoint Langley. He was one of the most respected scientists of his day, and human flight had become his passion. As a result, he had focused the extensive resources of the Smithsonian not only in money but also in personal expertise, to help solve the many problems associated with human powered flight. Langley's experiment in aerodynamics had been going on for over ten years and had finally led to the first unmanned powered flight on the Potomac River on May 6, 1896. Aerodrome #5, as it was called, was sixteen feet long with a wing on the front and another behind. It lifted off from a barge in the river propelled by a steam-driven engine. It made one slow circle before the engine stopped, and it crashed into the river. The engine they designed was gas powered and weighed 156 pounds. The transmission was simply chains running in tubes and then crossed to make the propellers revolve in opposite directions to counteract the torque.

The elusive dream of powered human flight was finally realized by Wilbur and Orville Wright on Dec 17, 1903, at Kill Devil Hills, North Carolina.

The results of their flights that day were as follows:

- 10:35 am .... Orville flew 120 feet in 12 seconds at 30 mph.

- 11:20 am .... Wilbur flew 175 feet in 12 seconds.
- 11:40 am .... Orville flew 200 feet in 15 seconds.
- 12:00 noon .... Wilbur flew 852 feet in 59 seconds.

In 1995, I made my first visit to Cape Kennedy. As I stood under the magnificent and overwhelming Saturn V rocket (the most powerful engine ever built) on display there, I reflected on how far we had come in just a short sixty-six years. From the first flight at Kitty Hawk on December 17, 1903, to the moon landing July 20, 1969.

A Comparison of the Two

	Wright Flyer	Apollo 11 Spacecraft
Weigh	605 pounds	6.5 million pounds
Length	40 feet 4 inches	363 feet
Horsepower	12	160 million
Speed	30 miles per hour	15,647 miles per hour
Distance traveled	120 feet	953,054 miles
Time	12 seconds	8 days

In 1927, a large monument was unveiled at Kill Devil Hills in Kitty Hawk, North Carolina. It commemorates the achievement of the Wright brothers and overlooks the spot where the first flights occurred. On the side of the monument are inscribed the following words: "CONCEIVED BY GENIUS...ACHIEVED BY DAUNTLESS RESOLUTION AND UNCONQUERABLE FAITH."

CHAPTER 5

"IT'S A CINCH BY THE INCH, AND A TRIAL BY THE MILE"

Patience / Perspective

"The journey of a thousand miles begins with a single step."

Lao Tzu

FOLLOWING A DEVASTATING EXPLOSION aboard Apollo 13 as it was traveling on its mission of landing on the moon in July of 1970, the crew realized that they were running out of fuel and breathable air, they were 210,000 miles from home, they were on a ship, and that ship was dying. After losing the Apollo 13 shot of reaching the moon, the crew was attempting to simply stay alive.

"We have 1,200 things to do, and we are only on number six. Focus on the first."

Jim Lovell, *Lost Moon*

Dad would often say, "I don't care how fast you are moving but I do care in what direction you are going. First, decide what it is you really want in life, and then figure out what it is going to take to get there. The world will step aside for the young man who knows where he is going." And then he would add, "There is always room for the best."

He rarely asked how quickly I was going to get there. Life had taught him that the things that are really important just take time. I was not always so patient. My take on life has often been, "I want it, I want it all, and I want it all right now." And when that didn't happen, as was usually the case, anxiety and discouragement would again become my friends. This was usually the time that Dad would step in and remind me that life doesn't have to be so complicated. It can really be quite simple. We just need to take everything a step at a time. This is where he would remind me, "Son, It's a cinch by the inch, and a trial by the mile."

Dad always refused to quit or admit defeat, regardless of how challenging the task at hand seemed to appear. He would decide what it was he wanted to do and then break it down into manageable components. He understood that often the task at hand might be overwhelming or just too daunting, so he often reminded me to pace myself and not expect everything to happen on what was often an unrealistic schedule and an improbable outcome. He would often say, "Sometimes during difficult periods in our lives when we feel we just can't take it anymore, sometimes in order to survive, it becomes necessary to take life just one day at a time, or maybe it will be just getting through the next hour, or possibly even just the next ten minutes."

It was early morning, and the Grand Canyon was beginning to come to life. The sound of the river created a soothing rhythm, much like the waves of the ocean as they crash against the shore, except that here on the Colorado River, those waves are called "rapids." Some crested as high as twenty feet. The sun was just beginning to paint the sheer cliffs rising above us a brilliant red, a passive pink and a golden yellow. The river had been a muddy brown the day before, but this particular morning it was running a deep emerald green.

I had often heard tales of Georgie, the old woman of the river. I felt they had all been greatly exaggerated until that morning. As soon as I laid eyes on her, I instantly believed them all. There she was in the middle of her triple pontoon boat, her hair coarse and standing out in every direction, her face a dark tan like the leather of an old horse saddle. And yes, she was wearing those leopard leotards that she was so famous for. She had been a constant as a guide on the Colorado River for the past forty years. Most boats plying the rapids of the Colorado through the Grand Canyon were either wooden dories, eight-man rafts or large rafts fashioned after World War II surplus pontoon boats. Prior to the use of these large rubber rafts, the number of people able to run the Colorado through the Grand Canyon had been limited to a total of just around one hundred. Following the introduction of the inflatable boat, that number rose rapidly to thousands each month. A typical raft was like an elongated oval, twelve feet wide and forty feet long. For stability, a forty-foot pontoon tube was attached to each side. A single raft could hold around eighteen people with all their supplies for a twelve-day trip. But Georgie's raft was three pontoon boats tied together side by side. It was like watching an aircraft carrier coming down the river. The one advantage with her trips was that there was not a chance in the world she was ever going to flip over. Our single pontoon boats could not make the same claim. It was not long after Georgie had passed by that we shoved off for the day.

Two separate boats and thirty-six people. The first rapid we would come to that morning at mile forty-four was called "President Harding." The scale of judging the severity of rapids across the country ranges from one to six, with six being the most difficult to maneuver. The Colorado River, along with a few others in North America, often uses a scale from one to ten-plus. President Harding was a four. It was our second day out and with little thought, we started down the mighty river. I watched in disbelief as our sister boat in front of us hit the President Harding Rapid and did a slow roll that ended with the boat upside down and everyone in the river, with some trapped underneath. It took about three miles before we could get the boat into a small eddy and rescue the people trapped in air pockets underneath the boat. I asked Mark, the main guide, what our options were. I was informed that the trip was now over. We could not turn the boat back over. The total weight of the boat and equipment exceeded four tons. The boat would remain upside down with all the equipment now suspended under the boat and at the mercy of the river. All the passengers would be placed on the good boat, and we would tow the damaged boat behind. In four days, we would reach a place in the canyon where helicopters could land to evacuate everyone out. We would then travel for another four days to Lake Mead, and in the marina, get a crane to lift the damaged boat along with its cargo, or what might be left of it, out of the water on to dry land.

A lot of people had paid good money to have the experience of a lifetime. I didn't own the river running company, I was just going along to help a friend of mine, who happened to be one of the guides. But for some strange reason I felt responsible, or at least I felt I might be able to make a difference, and I wasn't about to give up so easily.

After getting everyone accounted for and safely on shore, we tied up the boat in a small eddy and began to unpack the food, equipment and supplies from under the overturned boat. We would cut the straps holding everything in place and the containers and duffel bags would drop into the riverbed. We would then form a line and retrieve everything we could reach, one sleeping bag or one can of soup at a time, until we had salvaged most of what was underwater.

We removed the side pontoons, deflated three chambers on one side of the boat, and with ropes tied over and under the remaining inflated portions of the boat, and with the help of about forty people from other boats coming down the river who stopped to help, we were able to flip the boat over and repair and re-inflate the damaged chambers. We then re-rigged the boat with the supplies and equipment we had salvaged, and eight hours later we were on our way again.

On the boat that had overturned was a man from Minnesota. He had brought his wife and four kids, ages seventeen to twenty-five, out to run the river. After the boat capsized, he wanted to be immediately evacuated out of the canyon. No one was hurt, but he was just terribly shaken by the incident. There was only one problem. Because of the sheer walls and the fact that you were over a mile down inside the canyon, there was no line of sight to call out. The only chance of getting help was to catch the frequency of a commercial airline that might be passing directly overhead and ask the pilot to send help. Our second option would be to get help at Phantom Ranch at mile 89 where there would be a landline phone available

Phantom Ranch has a small store and some cabins for people to stay in who are hiking from the rim down to the river. It's at Phantom Ranch that three trails intersect: The Bright Angel Trail and the Kaibab Trail from the south rim and North Kaibab Trail from the north rim. In 1935, a bridge was built at Phantom Ranch so hikers and mules could cross the Colorado River.

While we were working on getting the boat operable again, the frightened father sat on the shore trying to process what had just happened, when one of the guides from one of the boats that had stopped to help us came over and sat down next to him. The guide was in his mid-forties and reminded me of Robinson Crusoe: long hair, a beard, well-tanned from years of running the river, with a vocabulary that contained more cuss words than complete sentences.

The conversation then went as follows (I have left out the swear words because I don't have the space or inclination to write them all down. And besides, I don't even know how to spell some of them.):

"I understand you were on that raft that flipped. Wow what a ride, you might have to pay extra for the experience." The man responded, "Well, actually it was terrible, and we are all going home as soon as we can get out of here."

The guide then looked at him with that stare which said, "Are you &#%$ serious?"

He continued, "You're telling me that you're going to take your kids out of here just as it's starting to get exciting. Well, all I can say is, if you're leaving here, be sure to take that big yellow stripe that's running down your back with you. As I see it, you can play this one of two ways, you can go back now, and by going home early, you teach your kids that you always fold when it gets hard. Then when people ask how your trip was, you can say, 'The boat flipped and I got wet and I was really scared, so I ran back home.' Or by staying, you can say, 'The second day out, our forty-foot raft flipped upside down in the middle of President Harding Rapid. We were trapped under the boat and survived in small air pockets, and it took a long time to get free, but we survived, repaired the four-ton boat and got it floating again. Then we continued on this great adventure deep into the Grand Canyon on one of the mighty rivers in the world.' Then each time you tell the story you will add new details, and it will only get better and better. But the choice is yours. You can be the hero or the frightened child." The guide did such a number on the man that he really had no option except to stay. He did make one demand, and that was when we hit Crystal Rapids, usually a ten-plus, that he be let out of the boat to walk around the rapid, to which my friend Mark (the guide) readily agreed. After the man walked away, I turned to Mark and said, "I didn't think you could walk around Crystal. I didn't realize there was a trail." Mark responded, "Your right, there isn't one. But at that point of the river there is no going back — he will just have to run it."

Fixing the raft using a crane (the trial by the mile) seemed the only option, and yet the solution came in a much more simplified way: a cinch by the inch.

Historical

Building of the Transcontinental Railroad and *Hell on Wheels*

The idea of building a transcontinental railroad (starting in 1864) was overwhelming in its scope and design.

The route would start near Omaha, Nebraska and end in Sacramento, California,1,776 miles away. The Union Pacific railroad started near Omaha and moved west while the Central Pacific started in Sacramento and headed east. They would survey the route, level the grade, blast out fifteen tunnels through the Sierra Nevada Range, along with thirty-seven miles of snow tunnels, build hundreds of wooden trestle bridges or fill in gorges and ravines with dirt. Each railroad employed as many as 15,000 workers at any one time.

A large part of the Union Pacific workforce were Irish immigrants while a vast majority of the Central Pacific came from China.

To complete the 1,776 miles of track, 1,086 miles by the Union Pacific Railroad and 690 miles by the Central Pacific, they would have to lay down:

- 4,582,080   Wooden railroad ties
- 625,152   Steel rails weighing 568 pounds each
- 9,768,000   Spikes to hold the rails to the ties (three taps of the hammer per spike)
- 1,250,304   Fishplates
- 2,500,608   Bolts, washers, and nuts to connect the rails to each other

All were done by hand with wheelbarrows, shovels, sledgehammers, axes, crow bars, blasting powder, and horse drawn scrapers along with a lot of blood, sweat, and tears.

It would seem an insurmountable task, but by breaking it down into small components, there was the possibility that it could be done — one railroad tie at a time, and one spike driven at a time. In the Sierra Nevada, where the mountains became too steep to go over or too large to go around, it became necessary to blast tunnels through them. Progress some days might be measured in feet or yards. Other days, six inches of blasting would be considered a success.

Until the building of the Panama Canal in the early part of the twentieth century, one of the great engineering feats of the modern world was the construction of the Transcontinental Railroad. In 1859, if someone wanted to travel from New York to California, their options were arduous and demanding. You could either procure a wagon and a team of oxen to pull it, buy a horse, or walk, which is what a vast majority of those early settlers ended up doing because a totally outfitted wagon could cost upwards of $1,000. The journey from New York to Sacramento was over 2,800 miles, and it would take the average traveler about three months to complete. Ten years later, with the completion of the Transcontinental Railroad, the same journey would cost as little as $70 and take just seven days.

This construction project in its entirety would be beyond the ability to comprehend. It became necessary to break it up into small manageable components. Instead of designing one large project taking the line from St. Louis west to the Pacific Coast, it was divided into two manageable components. The Union Pacific would start near Omaha, Nebraska and move west, while the Central Pacific would start in Sacramento, California and head east across the Rockies. The more difficult of the two rested with the Central Pacific. The Union Pacific laid track on relatively flat land until they reached the Rocky Mountains, while the Central had to deal with steep grades, blasting tunnels through mountains, building trestles across ravines and valleys, and dealing with severe weather, especially in winter where snowfall often exceeded sixteen feet deep.

The Civil War, with all its tragic consequences, prepared the country to accomplish such a great feat. From the war came the ability to mass produce large quantities of supplies, such as railroad ties, rails, spikes, and dynamite, motivating leadership and men who knew how to take orders and work for a common goal, 32,000 at any given time. The undertaking also required the ability to transport, house, and feed men and equipment, 1,776 miles over mountains and ravines, and to stage the work in a different location every day. Everyone was required to work under extreme conditions, not only in freezing snow and stifling heat, but for long hours and with very poor food. The financing for such an undertaking required creating at that time the two largest corporations in America: the Central Pacific Railroad Co. and The Union Pacific Railroad Co. The real heroes were the men working at the same task day after day, mile after exhausting mile. One spike driver, three taps, 21,000,000 times.

Life was not easy on the frontier. Salt Lake City was the only town between St. Louis and Sacramento, so a traveling tent city of approximately two to four thousand inhabitants accompanied the workers. As the work moved forward, so would the town. It soon had its own well-deserved name: "Hell on Wheels." Its sole purpose for existence was to see how quickly it could separate a working man from his wages.

"'These places were built of the most perishable materials,' wrote Samuel Bowles, editor of a newspaper called *The Springfield Republican*. 'They consisted of canvas tents, plain board shanties, and turf-hovels. A few variety stores and shops, and many grogs-shops; by day disgusting, by night dangerous; almost everybody dirty, many filthy, and with marks of lowest vice, averaging a murder a day; gambling and drinking, hurdy-gurdy dancing, and the vilest of sexual commerce the chief business and pastime of the hours.'"

Postscript

The competitive spirit was alive and well, even after four years of intensive and exhausting labor. The biggest bragging rights would go to the workers who could lay down the longest section of track in one day. In 1868, the men of the Union Pacific laid down four and one-half miles. The Central Pacific, not to be outdone, countered with six miles and a few feet, only to be beat again by the Union Pacific, completing eight miles plus. It was decided by Crocker of the Central Pacific that the only way to hold the ultimate record would be to wait until the very end of construction. On April 27, 1869, the Union Pacific was within eight miles of Promontory Summit and the Central Pacific had fourteen miles to go. If the Central Pacific crew laid down ten miles of track, there would be no way the Union Pacific could then beat them.

"What the Central Pacific did that day will be remembered as long as this republic lasts. White men born in America were there, along with former slaves whose ancestors came from Africa, plus immigrants from all across Europe, and more than three thousand Chinamen. There were some Mexicans with at least a touch of Native American blood in them, as well as French Indians and at least a few Native Americans. Everyone was excited, ready to get to work, eager to show what he could do. Even the Chinese, usually methodical and a bit scornful of the American way of doing things, were stirred to a fever pitch. They and all the others. We are the world, they said. They had come together at this desolate place in the middle of Western North America to do what had never been done before them. They moved the track forward at the rate of almost a mile an hour. They laid at a rate of approximately 240 feet every seventy-five seconds."

Stephen Ambrose,
Nothing Like it in the World

Thirteen days later on May 10, 1869, the driving of the golden spike at Promontory Point, Utah, signaled the completion of this extraordinary endeavor.

CHAPTER 6

"YOU CAN'T MAKE A SILK PURSE OUT OF A SOW'S EAR ...OR CAN YOU?"

Creativity

"All of our dreams can come true if we have the courage to pursue them."

Walt Disney

I CAN STILL HEAR DAD'S words resonating in my ears: "See what others cannot, use your imagination to turn the ordinary into something extraordinary. Think outside the box." And so I have tried my whole life to do just that. Dad took us on a lot of journeys of discovery, and I have tried to do the same with my kids.

T-Rex chasing after a Triceratops, a Brontosaurus standing on its hind legs to reach three stories into the sky where the tender leaves awaited. It stirs wonder and awe in the mind of a small child, and I consider myself a small child in more ways than one. To visit the exact spot that these marvelous creatures once called home, where they were born, lived, and died, seemed to me a marvelous journey. I didn't have to do much of a sales job to convince our kids to tag along on this journey traveling back in time millions of years. The only challenge we faced was to keep four little kids entertained as we traveled the 160 miles to Fossil Butte National Monument located in the flatlands of Wyoming. It was made a national monument in 1972. The National Parks Foundation calls Fossil Butte National Monument a "fifty-million-year-old lakebed with one of the richest fossil localities in the world."

Many of the specimens are found in museums worldwide Most of the fossils are fish, insects, plants, reptiles, birds and mammals." No T-Rexs, a small oversite on my part, but the kids didn't need to know that. We decided it would be easier if we broke the "expedition" up into a series of manageable segments. First stop, ice cream cones in Logan, second stop, bathroom to clean up the ice cream from Logan, which now decorated three of the four kids. Question: how can a kid have more ice cream on his clothes than the volume of what was originally purchased? Third stop, Bear Lake, located in a high mountain valley in the Ashley National Forest. This pristine lake has the most beautiful deep blue color imaginable. Had I been a little smarter, I easily could have bypassed stop number two, the bathroom, and just waited to throw the kids in the lake instead. I realized they were going into the lake anyway. By the way, what is it with rocks and water? It appears to be a rite of passage that kids (and most adults acting like kids) have this innate need to find every available rock that is not too heavy to lift and throw them into the nearby lake until all the rocks are gone or the lake is full, whichever comes first. Stop four, lunch in Evanston, Wyoming. Stop five, back to the lake to throw the kids in again. The same question arises: how can a child end up with more food on his or her clothes than the volume of what was originally purchased? Question: is there any way we can just take part of the lake with us to avoid bathroom stops?

By the time we got to Fossil Butte, Mom and Dad were tired and cranky, and the four kids were well rested, having slept the last hour of our expedition.

Years later, when one of our sons was in a geology class in high school, the teacher asked the following question: "Who in this class can tell me what Fossil Butte is?" My son's hand quickly went up, and then quickly came down (but not quite fast enough) when he realized he was the only one to respond. The teacher had seen it.

"Well BJ, how do you know what Fossil Butte is?"

"Because I have been there," came his sheepish reply.

"You have been there?" asked the teacher, somewhat surprised.

"Yes, with my family years ago."

"Well, this is a first," she said. "I have been teaching for over twenty-two years, and I have never had a single student who knew what it was, let alone met someone who has actually been there. Would you please tell the class about it."

"Well," he proceeded, "it's in the middle of Wyoming (it's not), which means you go to the end of the earth and then turn left. It's about one hundred miles from anything living. It once contained more fossils than any other place in the world, A lot of the fossils are gone now and all that remains is a big hole in the ground resembling a gravel pit. They have in the pit what looks like a double-wide trailer with a few small bones on display under an old glass counter, and that's about it."

This excursion has long since joined the one to ten scale, with number ten being Disneyland, and number one being Fossil Butte. It has been a running joke in the family. When I propose a trip, the question always asked is, "It's not like Fossil Butte, is it?"

The postscript to this adventure was the realization that although the destination was a bust for the kids, the journey was not. The kids had a great time eating ice cream, having a burger and fries, seeing some beautiful mountain scenery around Logan, Utah, and swimming in a vivid blue mountain lake.

Historical

Walt Disney — A creative visionary who gave us "The Happiest Place on Earth"

It was not only the high-pitched screams of absolute fear, but the wild commotion that followed that caught my attention. The sound of chairs being dragged across the kitchen floor, and little bodies clambering up on top of tables and counter tops, cups and silverware and cookbooks flying across the room in every direction. It all created a definite sense of total panic, and it had all occurred because of the unexpected appearance of one tiny little mouse, and a very frightened little mouse at that. Everyone was in retreat except petite little seven-year-old Anna. BJ was on the counter, Liz was on the table, and Steve was running for cover out of the dining room doorway. But it was Anna with a broom in hand that was charging into the frontline of the battle. The broom was much bigger than she was, but she was swinging it at our little intruder with the ferocity of a general on a mission to save his country. The little mouse finally found refuge out of the back door and into the yard. As the door slammed shut behind the vanquished foe, calm returned to the house, and all was back to normal. It was not long after that I noticed several of the kids sporting their Donald Duck shirts and Mickey Mouse ears heading out to play. Walt Disney had indeed created a silk purse out of a sow's ear. He had taken that small, insignificant rodent and turned it into one of the most loved and recognized figures of the last ninety years, and along with Mickey's meteoric rise came the success of the Disney Company. Revenues in 2022 were over $82 billion.

Walt excelled at taking those things we view as routine and ordinary and magically transforming them into something that we would come to love and cherish.

A simple mouse became Mickey.

Mickey's girlfriend became Minnie.

A bloodhound became Pluto.

Another vest-wearing dog, Dippy Dawg, would soon be known as Goofy.

A duck would become Donald.

Marceline, a small town in Missouri, became Main Street, USA.

A simple orange grove in Anaheim, California became the Magic Kingdom.

An empty grassland in Florida was turned into Disney World and the Epcot Center.

A simple camera was incorporated into a device that created a 3D effect in animation — the first of its kind.

Mickey: His Creation Would Become the Foundation of an Empire

There are several accounts of Mickey's origin, but no definitive record exists. One is that Walt saw a mouse caught in a garbage can next to his desk and was intrigued watching it trying to get out. Another was seeing a mouse scratching at his window trying to escape.

The first cartoon character Walt Disney came up with was Oswald the Lucky Rabbit. Disney had created the character, but Universal Pictures held the rights to it.

In March 1928, Walt went to New York to negotiate a better and more lucrative deal with Universal Pictures, but to no avail. It was on his return train ride back to his home in Los Angeles that Walt started to draw a likeness of a mouse on a piece of paper. He was twenty-six years old.

Mickey Mouse made his first appearance in a cartoon named *Plane Crazy* on May 15, 1928. It would be followed in November of that same year by something that was the first of its kind: a fully sound synchronized cartoon named *Steamboat Willie*. The cartoon was still showing in theaters a year later. Walt was Mickey's voice and would continue to be for almost another twenty years.

Walt took basically three circles and dressed it in yellow shoes, white gloves, and red shorts, and it became the most recognizable brand in history.

Walt Disney's Influence in the World

I think of what my childhood would have been had there been no Walt Disney. There would have been a lot of empty spaces.

What we have today because of him:

Mickey Mouse — 1928

Minnie Mouse

Pluto

Goofey

Donald Duck

ABC America

Davy Crockett

> Played by Fess Parker in 1955. Disney sold over $300 million in coonskin caps. watches, and lunch boxes. I vividly remember, because I was one of those young frontiersmen who just had to have one of those coonskin caps.

Mickey Mouse Club

Wonderful World of Disney

> We invited Uncle Walt into our homes every Sunday night. He became family.

Movies included:

> *Snow White and the Seven Dwarfs* (It took four years to make 1937.)

Pinocchio	1940
Fantasia	1940
Dumbo	1941
Bambi	1942 (They brought in a live fawn to practice drawing on.)
Cinderella	1950
Treasure Island	1950
Alice in Wonderland	1951
Peter Pan	1953
Lady and the Tramp	1955
Sleeping Beauty	1959
101 Dalmatians	1961
Mary Poppins	1964

Songs

"High Ho"

"Whistle While You Work"

"When You Wish Upon a Star"

Educational films such as:

> *Johnny Tremaine and the Sons of Liberty.* Johnny was a young man who joined a group called The Sons of

Liberty in 18th century Boston fighting for American independence in the Revolutionary War.

The main song in the movie is forever in my mind:

"Stand for the right of man, boys, stand against all tyranny, hang the lamp of freedom boys, high on the liberty tree....For we are the sons, yes we are the sons, the sons of liberty."

Walt Disney also pioneered

- Full color, three strip Technicolor
- Synchronized sound
- Perfected the rotating camera
- Animation with live action, as in *Fantasia*
- Multiplane camera

It moves the animated artwork across the camera lens at different speeds and distances from each other, giving the whole process a 3D look. The result is the appearance of depth, having the drawings move at different speeds and distances from the lens. You could now have moving water behind the main subject and could introduce changing light and shadows.

His most famous legacy was Disneyland. Walt Disney bought a 160-acre orange grove in Southern California and started construction in July 1954. It took one year to build and opened on July 17, 1955. They expected 15,000 people but over 25,000 showed up the first day. Traffic jams extended over seven miles, many of the drinking fountains didn't work, the temperature reached one-hundred degrees, high-heeled shoes sunk into the asphalt, and some of the rides broke down. Even with all the problems, Walt's vision was infectious, and the public was not deterred. Within ten weeks, over a million people had visited the park. Two years later, ten million people had come. It started with thirty-five rides and attractions and now has 101 rides and attractions with an average attendance of 51,000 people per day.

Disneyland was a place growing up that allowed us to escape into a world that we all wished actually existed. I personally loved the tall, masted sailing ship in the lagoon in Frontierland where you could buy a tuna fish sandwich with a small pirate sword stuck in the top, I only got the sandwich to get the sword. The Swiss Family Robinson tree house was my favorite. What kid wouldn't want to grow up on an island in the South Pacific where all you did all day was play? Main Street represented the town we all wanted to come from. It portrayed a time in American history that was safe, friendly, and wholesome. It was the same town that Walt portrayed in his movie, *The Music Man*, starring Debbie Reynolds as Marian the librarian, Robert Preston as Professor Harold Hill, and little Johnny played by a young Ronnie Howard. It was set in a small Midwestern town that loved parades, picnics, and the Fourth of July. A place where everyone knew and cared about each other.

Walt was a never-ending source of creativity that resulted in such iconic attractions as:

- Pirates of the Caribbean
- Jungle Cruise (The corny jokes never grow old.)
- The Matterhorn (More people can identify the ride than the original mountain in Switzerland.)
- Sleeping Beauty's Castle
- The Haunted Mansion
- The Monorail
- Mr. Toad's Wild Ride
- Abraham Lincoln (with animatronics bringing him to life)

Disney received twenty-two Academy Awards, the most in Academy history.

With the opening of Disney World in 1971 In Orlando, Florida, the comedian Bob Hope said, "This is the biggest vacation entertainment complex in the world. And to think it all started with a gentle mouse, a bad-tempered duck and seven mixed up dwarfs."

CHAPTER 7

"BRING ON ANOTHER MOUNTAIN"

Opposition / Growth

"In memories we are rich, we have suffered, starved, and triumphed, and we have seen God in all his splendor."

Ernest Shackleton

H E WAS A GIANT. Not a mean, angry giant, but a soft and gentle one. All my friends were afraid of him, but not me. He was 6 feet 6 inches tall and weighed well over 300 pounds. His shoes were huge — size 16 — and they reminded me of small boats. His hands were like baseball gloves. His voice was deep and booming, like distant thunder. And his eyes were blue and piercing, like the lightning that followed. There appeared to be nothing that he was afraid of. If he was, he never let it show. To everyone who knew him he was Big John. To me, he was simply Dad.

He was born a gentle and happy child, and through the years, with the trials and challenges of life, he also became strong, and wise, and kind. He came to understand that, without opposition in all of life's endeavors, there can be no real growth. Muscles aren't built sitting on a couch, wisdom is not gained if we fail to learn, and success is never realized without a lot of failures along the way.

The creed that Dad followed all his life was simple: "Bring on another mountain. And when I have climbed it, bring me another one, and make sure it is a little taller and a little steeper." He always taught that "challenges in life can provide one of two outcomes: a great opportunity to become stronger, or a platform for self-pity." Dad always chose the first. Even when he had a lot to complain about, he never went the self-pity route. It simply was not a part of his DNA.

Dad always loved a challenge. He rarely got discouraged, even when things did not go his way. He never complained about how tough things were. One fall morning, when my work took me to within a few miles of my parents' home, I had a free hour, so I decided to pay them a visit. Looking back now, I realize that I had my priorities backward. Scheduling a visit with the folks should have been my number one priority, and then if I had time, and work just happened to be close by, then fine. Work should have been second in importance. I have a lot of regrets in life, but probably one of my greatest is that I did not take more time to visit them. There are so many things I would have loved to talk to them about. If I could turn the clock back, I would want to know more about Mom's life as a little girl growing up on a farm in rural Idaho. I would like to know why Teddy Roosevelt was one of Dad's heroes, and why he thought Harry Truman was a good president. But those opportunities are now gone and can never be retrieved.

Going to see the folks always brightened my day. I would always be greeted at the door with a smile from ear to ear, followed by a huge bear hug, accompanied by, "Oh what a wonderful surprise, It is so good to see you. Come in. Are you hungry? Can we get you something to eat?" That would be followed by a litany of questions: "How are the kids? How is work going?" My response was usually the same: "No I'm not hungry, the kids are fine and work is okay." Eventually the conversation came around to Dad's health. On one particular visit, I mentioned that he (Dad) looked a little on the tired side, He responded very calmly, "Well, son, I had a doctor's appointment this morning and was told I have terminal bone cancer." Telling me that news was almost an afterthought to him. Here I was in tears, my world had just been turned upside down, and yet there was Dad showing no more emotion than a shrug of the shoulders. When I asked why he wasn't a wreck like I had instantly become, his response was classic Dad. "Son, it's not exactly what I would have asked for, but since these are the cards I have been dealt, then these are the cards I will play. Life goes on." Over the next few months, it was hard to watch his decline. The man who had always been so tall, now stood with drooping shoulders. The voice that was strong now had become a soft whisper, his long walking stride was reduced to a mere shuffle. Even in the last few weeks of his life as the pain became horrific and the light in his eyes was slowly fading, his indomitable spirit never did.

The last month of his life when he was pretty much confined to a wheelchair, I would push him up and down the streets by his home. As we passed each house, the neighbors would see him coming. They would drop everything to come out to spend time with Dad, even if it was just a brief minute. They all realized that this might be their last opportunity to hear his voice, see his heartfelt smile and especially to get one more big hug from a man they knew really cared about them. Dad was genuinely interested in each and every person he ever met. His response was always the same. Instead of focusing on his own wretched state, he would quickly deflect the conversation from himself to the person he was talking to:

"Mark, how is your son doing in Virginia?"

"Carol, I sure hope your kids are feeling better."

"Joe, I understand your daughter is getting married. That's wonderful. Please give her my best."

In his entire life, it was never about Big John, it was always about others. You never left Dad's presence without feeling better about yourself, and knowing he really cared about you and that his love was genuine. The man he had become was the result of all the mountains he had learned to climb. A life filled with challenges; a life well lived.

I have tried to emulate his example in the way I treat other people. I guess I am still learning how to climb the mountain of compassion, because occasionally I find it really hard to care about certain individuals. I try to look for the good in everyone, but sometimes they give me pause. I have learned over time what dad had tried to teach me: that regardless of how hard a person might be to love, there are redeeming qualities in every single individual. Sometimes we just need to look a little deeper to find them.

I have experienced challenges in my own life, and I have often reflected back on Dad's example in order to work through them. Some are just small hills to get over, while others seem to tower so high that I can't see the top of the peaks. They are obscured in the clouds of uncertainty and doubt.

Two events in my own life have put me at the base of the tallest mountains I believe I will ever have to climb. They both involved the heart.

The one mountain that is my personal Everest (that I am still trying to summit) came years ago when I experienced a broken heart with the loss of my youngest son, Eric. He was ten at the time of his death. He was really quite an incredible kid. When I came home from work each night, he would be the first to run out to my truck to meet me. He would jump up into my arms and give me a big bear hug. When he was four years old, he requested for his birthday a wheelbarrow because Dad had one, and he wanted to be just like Dad. He was extremely competitive with his four brothers, and he always had to be the winner in every race, or the first one done with their chores. When his oldest sister Liz was recovering from a serious car accident, Eric slept in a sleeping bag on the floor next to her bed for nearly a month so that if she needed anything in the middle of the night, he would be there for her. With Eric's death, I felt as if my whole world had come crumbling down around me. I often felt a tremendous pressure in my chest making it hard to even breathe. The whole experience and sense of loss was so profound that even to this day words cannot begin to describe the feelings of sadness that can still arise. Occasionally I will be driving along, and suddenly something around me — a sight, or a song on the radio, or a smell — will trigger past emotions, and I find tears running down my cheeks. I will pull over and have a good little cry, wipe the tears off my face, take a deep breath, calm down, and then drive on, feeling a little better. When other people I have known have lost a child, I thought I could empathize with them. Certainly, I could imagine what It might have felt like if I had lost one of my own kids. But oh, I could not have been more wrong. Until a parent actually goes through this terrible ordeal, they can't possibly understand the tremendous sense of loss. A loss this deep has caused me to reflect on life's priorities — what is truly important and what is not. Everything that was so important on June 30, meant absolutely nothing on July 1, the day he died. Since Eric's death, I have radically changed my priorities. My family ties mean everything to me. I refuse to miss significant events in their lives. Often it is not convenient to fly home early from a work trip or miss an important meeting in order to attend a dance recital or a soccer game. But it is worth every effort. My seven kids and thirty grandchildren can never say that Dad (Grandpa) does not care. I believe they all know how much I love them.

The second-tallest mountain I have had to climb came in October, several years ago. I experienced another broken heart: cardiomyopathy (a weak heart muscle), which led to sudden cardiac arrest. If two of my sons had not been by my side to administer CPR when it happened, and if the paramedics had not been so close, I would not be here today. With the severity of my cardiomyopathy, I was told my chances of survival were about one percent. I now carry a pacemaker and a defibrillator in my chest. It has taken several years to return to a somewhat normal life with the medications and pacemaker.

Climbing this mountain has again provided a powerful reminder to me of what is truly important and added a second course correction to my life: that of gratitude. I have become extremely grateful for even the smallest of things. I greet every day with such profound joy that I am still here. I marvel at every single sunrise and sunset. The beauty of a small flower or leaves on a tree is exciting. People smiling, kids laughing. Even when the wind is blowing outside and the temperature is below zero, it is still a beautiful day, and I am grateful for having been given just one more day to enjoy this incredible world that we have the privilege to live in.

The heart I possess today, I attribute mostly to my father. I am who I am, because of him.

I asked Dad shortly before he passed away, "Dad, if you had your life to live over again, what would you change?" I wish I had never posed that question because his answer bothered me for a long time. He said, "Son I would not have changed a single thing, I loved every minute of my life, and I would live it all over again just the same."

The reason I did not like his response is because I thought if I had my life to live over again, I would change a lot of things. How rare it was, I thought, to have lived such an idyllic life. Years later, as I contemplated his answer, it occurred to me that his life was not perfect. It came with great challenges and disappointments that he would have preferred not to have gone through. But by the same token, he had charted a course that gave him joy and a sense of fulfillment, and the general direction he had chosen was one he loved. He had climbed many mountains and had gained an elevated perspective of life. I have since come to the conclusion that if I were given a second chance to go back and change the course of my life, I would probably feel the same way Dad did. I would, however, try to avoid the fight I had with Glen Johnson when I was twelve. He really took me to the cleaners.

The following story has really given me perspective. When we feel that our lives are too hard, that we cannot go another day or even another step, this story reassures me that we can.

Historical

Ernest Shackleton — The greatest story of human survival against all odds

---

MEN WANTED FOR HAZARDOUS JOURNEY

Small wages
Bitter cold
Long months of complete darkness
Constant dangers
Safe return doubtful
Honor and recognition in case of success

This ad reportedly appeared in a London paper in 1914. It inspired over 5,000 men and three women to apply. The man who placed the ad was Ernest Shackleton. He would eventually choose just twenty-six men (and one stowaway) to accompany him on what was to become one of the most epic survival stories of all time.

The ship that was to carry twenty-eight men into the pages of history was ironically called the *Endurance*. It was one of the finest wooden ships ever built, and it had to be. Its mission was to carry men and supplies to the Antarctic in an attempt to cross the continent on foot, from west to east.

Ernest Shackleton had become a national hero upon his return to England in 1907. Even though the expedition under his leadership had failed in its attempt to be the first to reach the South Pole, the fact that he had made a valiant attempt had endeared him to the people of his native land. Shackleton and three companions had made it to within ninety-seven miles of their goal before a shortage of food and supplies forced them to turn back. The prize of being the first to reach the South Pole was eventually claimed by a Norwegian named Roald Amundsen in December 1911. Amundsen had reached the South Pole just thirty days ahead of Robert F. Scott, a fellow countryman and personal friend of Shackleton. Scott and three of his companions perished on the ice before they could return to their base camp.

For Shackleton, his dream of becoming the first man to reach the South Pole had now vanished. But he refused to admit defeat. Instead, he channeled all his efforts into a new passion, adventure, and dream. To his wife, Emily Shackleton, he wrote, "I feel that another expedition, unless it crosses the continent, is not much." Shackleton longed for the glory, excitement, and prestige he had experienced in 1907. In an effort to raise money for his new monumental undertaking, he organized the Imperial Trans-Antarctic Expedition, and in a prospectus to raise money, he wrote, "From the sentimental point of view, it is the last great polar journey that can be made. It will be a greater journey than the journey to the Pole and back, and I feel that it is up to the British nation to accomplish this, for we have been beaten at the conquest of the North Pole (claimed by Admiral Robert E. Peary, an American, in 1909) and beaten at the first conquest of the South Pole. There now remains the largest and most striking of all journeys: the crossing of the continent."

The Man

Describing Shackleton, Alfred Lansing wrote, "He was above all, an explorer in the classic mold, utterly self-reliant, romantic, and just a little swashbuckling. He was now forty years old, of medium height and thick of neck, with broad, heavy shoulders a trifle stooped, and dark brown hair parted in the center. He had a wide, sensuous but expressive mouth that could curl into a laugh or tighten into a thin fixed line with equal facility. His jaw was like iron. His gray blue eyes, like his mouth, could come alight with fun or darken into a steely and frightening gaze. His face was handsome, though it often wore a brooding expression. He had small hands, but his grip was strong and confident. Whatever his mood — whether it was gay and breezy, or dark with rage — he had one pervading characteristic: he was purposeful."

Alfred Lansing,
Endurance

The monumental challenges that were to come would require all of his capabilities and more.

The Crew

The crew consisted of Shackleton and twenty-seven other men: a second-in-command, a captain, a first officer, a navigator, second and third officers, two engineers, two surgeons, a geologist, a meteorologist, a physicist, a biologist, an official photographer, an official artist, a motor expert, a carpenter, a cook, two firemen, five able seamen, and one stowaway.

The Ship

The ship was built in Sandefjord, Norway by the Framnaes Shipyard. It was a beautiful ship with three masts and built to the highest standards of the time. She was 144 feet long with a twenty-four-foot beam. Her keel consisted of four pieces of solid oak one laid on top of the other until it was seven feet thick. The outside was covered in planking to protect her from the sea. Her sides consisted of oak and Norwegian mountain fir, eighteen inches thick in some areas and up to two and a half feet in others. The outside of the planking was covered with sheeting, which consisted of greenheart, a wood that was so heavy it outweighed solid Iron. Regular tools were ineffective in shaping it. The bow, which would face the brunt of the ice pack, was built also of solid oak over four feet thick.

The Story

The expedition sailed from South Georgia Island on December 5, 1914. Six days later, they entered the pack ice of the Weddel Sea. By the following October, the men found themselves caught in the ice, and the ship that had been their home for the last ten months was slowly being crushed. The men would eventually have to abandon the ship and find a way to survive on the ice with no hope of rescue. The last man left the *Endurance* at 5 p.m. on October 27, 1915. It would not be long before the great ship would slip below the pack and disappear from sight. The men were now totally alone and on their own. The nearest inhabited outpost was 1,200 miles away and it would be a long time before anyone even knew that the crew of the *Endurance* was in trouble. It would be impossible to know even where to look for them if they had. If Shackleton and his men were to survive, it would now be totally up to them. Help would never come. They were stranded in one of the most inhospitable places on earth, where the winds could reach 180 miles per hour, and the temperatures could drop below minus eighty. In the arctic summers, it was light around the clock, and in the winter, there was never-ending darkness that could easily bring on a sense of loneliness, melancholy and depression that could be debilitating. The men rarely experienced relief from the constant cold and were seldom dry. Even their sleeping bags were cold and damp.

The nearest land mass from the pack ice was 182 miles away.

For the next five months, the men would camp on the ice in what they called "Camp Pationco," with tents as their only shelter from the extreme wind and frigid cold. If they were to survive, they would need to pull sleds of supplies while dragging three lifeboats across the pack ice in an attempt to reach open water where they could then navigate to the nearest land mass, Elephant Island. The men would survive on what rations they had salvaged before the ship sank, and when that grew scarce, they survived on seal meat and used blubber as their source of fuel for cooking. The smell was bad, but the strong black smoke was worse. After fifteen months of being stranded on the ice, they finally reached open water and headed for Elephant Island in the three small lifeboats they had pulled across the ice. By the time the men reached the island, they had been stranded for 497 days. Elephant Island was small and barren and could only be used as a stepping stone to go on. It was soon decided that Shackleton, along with five of his men, would put to sea in the *James Canard*, one of the small lifeboats. It is almost inconceivable to imagine that they would attempt such a feat. Six men in a twenty-two-foot lifeboat, starting an 800-mile journey that would take seventeen days in the open ocean. They would have to cross one of the most treacherous bodies of water in the world — the Weddel Sea — in a perilous attempt to reach South Georgia Island. If their navigational calculations were off even by a fraction of one degree, they would pass right by the island and not even know it. If they missed South Georgia Island, there would be nothing beyond to save them. They had only one shot, and they knew it.

When they finally made landfall, they were on the wrong side of the island. In order to reach the whaling station, it would require a trek of over thirty miles crossing a snow-covered range of mountains rising to over 7,000 feet. Shackleton and two of his men would make the crossing. The men were now wearing clothing that was not only water soaked but threadbare, and in addition to that, the men were far beyond exhaustion and weak from lack of food. Amazingly, they would accomplish this last great feat in just thirty-six hours. When they descended from the mountains, they were met by a Norwegian whaler who led them to the station manager's home. "Their faces were gray with blubber smoke, their hair matted with salt, and their clothing in tatters. "Who are you?" asked the station manager. The man said quietly, "Shackleton." The station manager turned away and wept.

Shackleton's Antarctic Adventure
— IMAX movie

Three attempts were made in the next four months to get a ship back to Elephant Island to rescue Shackleton's remaining twenty-two men. But each time the Weddel Sea proved to be far too treacherous even for larger ships. Again and again, they were forced to turn back. Finally, on August 30, 1916, they succeeded. What great joy must have filled Shackleton's heart as he neared Elephant Island to hear his men on shore shouting that all twenty-two men were still alive.

Shackleton's reflection on this incredible ordeal was expressed in the following statement by him:

"In memories we are rich,
We have suffered, starved, and triumphed,
We have seen God in all his splendor
We have heard the text that nature renders
We have reached the soul of man."

Shackleton died on January 5, 1922, and he was laid to rest on South Georgia Island. He was forty-seven years old.

CHAPTER 8

"TAKE CARE OF THE CORNERS, AND THE MIDDLE WILL TAKE CARE OF ITSELF"

Attention to small details

"It's the little things that make the big things possible."

J.W. Marriott,
founder of the Marriott Corporation,
parent company of the world's largest hotel chain

WHEN I WAS TWELVE years old, I had two big aspirations: one was to be able to play basketball every single day, and the other was to have my own 10-speed bicycle. If you had a 10-speed bike, you were living the dream. I didn't have the money needed to purchase one, so I approached my father for a donation to my cause. Dad was never one to give handouts — charitable donations yes, freebies no — but it was worth a try. True to form, the response was what I expected. "I won't just give you the money, but I will provide an opportunity for you to earn it." That was code for, "Get to work and make something of yourself."

One of the odd jobs he had in mind for me was to mop the kitchen floor, whereupon he agreed to pay me two dollars. That was pretty decent money back in those days, so I readily agreed. The kitchen was small, and I knew I could get the job done in a matter of minutes. I filled the bucket, took the mop, and in under five minutes I was done, easy money. A few minutes later found me at Dad's side to collect my earnings. "I finished mopping the floor and I'm here to get paid," I said. I was somewhat surprised by his response. "Well, son, you have already been paid." When I questioned him as to just how that happened, he took me back into the kitchen. "I left your money on the kitchen floor so you could be paid as you worked. The money you should have found is yours to keep as your pay." He had placed fifty cents in each corner of the kitchen, and I was in such a hurry that I had failed to find a single one. He then taught me a valuable lesson. He said, "Son, take care of the corners, and the middle will take care of itself. If you pay attention to the small details in everything you do, you will find that the larger issues and challenges in life tend to fall into place." I have since learned that when I ignore the small and simple things, they tend to add up until they become big problems that in many cases are followed by failure.

"The gates of history turn on small hinges, and so do people's lives. The choices we make determine our destiny."

Thomas S Monson

We often find that the time and distance between first and second place can be very, very small. Roger Bannister from Great Britain was the first man to break the four-minute mile on May 6, 1954. Two months later, John Landy of Australia accomplished the same feat. The world remembers the name Roger Bannister, but very few know who John Landy was.

Almost everyone in the world knows that Neil Armstrong was the first man to walk on the moon, but very few can name who the second man was.

The 1992 Summer Olympic Games were held in Barcelona, Spain. The gold medal in the 100-meter women's race was won by Gail Deavers of the United States. Her teammate, Gwen Torence, did not medal — she finished in fourth place. The difference between first and fourth place was a mere 3/100 of a second.

Small things really do matter.

Historical

D-Day invasion — The largest and most complex military operation in history Normandy, France WW II

At 10:56 p.m. on June 5, 1944, six Halifax bombers, each towing a Horsa glider, took off from Tarrant Rushton Airfield in southern England near the town of Exeter. They were part of the largest invasion force the world had ever known. The targets of this vast military force were the beaches of Normandy and the liberation of France, and then the rest of Europe. The German occupying force had now held the French people captive for over 1,435 days.

The six Horsa gliders were the tip of the spear and would be the first to land in France. Their commander was a 31-year-old major by the name of John Howard, who was part of the British contingency.

To fly a Horsa glider was much the same as piloting a plane, except you had no engine and therefore no room for mistakes. One shot to land, and that was it. The gliders were built by the British, starting in 1940. Metal was scarce, and so it was necessary to build wooden gliders. They were built in southern England, and by the end of the war, over 700 had been manufactured. The entire plane was built of wood with few exceptions, even the controls. It was a high wing monoplane, the nose was made of plexiglass, and the landing gear consisted of three wheels, two up front and one behind. The wings were eighty-eight feet wide, the fuselage was sixty-seven feet long, and it was capable of holding a pilot, a copilot, and either twenty-eight men fully armed, or two jeeps, a 75-mm Howitzer or a quarter-ton truck.

A total of156,000 men from Britain, Canada, and the United States would be landing on the beaches in Normandy France with assigned names such as Sword, Gold, Omaha, Utah, and Juno. Major Howard and his men had a more obscure target: Some five miles inland behind enemy lines near the town of Benouville. What made their mission so critical to the success of the invasion was reflected in the orders they had received just a few weeks earlier: "Your task is to seize intact the bridges over the Orne River and canal (Pegasus Bridge) at Benouville and to hold them until relief. The capture of the bridges will be a Coup de Main operation, depending largely on surprise, speed and dash for success, provided the bulk of your force lands safely."

These two bridges were of critical strategic importance, The Germans had rigged the bridges to blow them up if they were to ever fall into Allied hands. Without these two bridges, the invading force would not be able to move inland off the beaches, and the entire operation would be in grave danger of failing.

The challenges facing Major Howard were many. After being towed by the Halifax Bombers across the English Chanel, the tow line would be cut and they would then be on their own to land the bulky gliders within yards of their target, to do it in the dark of night and to do it totally undetected. They would be the first soldiers to land on German-occupied French soil in the early morning hours of that fateful day. He and his men were to overtake German positions fighting through anti-tank emplacement, pill boxes, barbed wire, machine gun nests and bunkers in order to secure two bridges. Both bridges had been wired by the Germans to detonate in case of an invasion by the Allied forces. Pegasus Bridge was over a large canal, and a nearby bridge spanned the Orne River.

In 1942, Howard was chosen to command a selected group of men for a mission yet to be disclosed but which required incredible preparation. Training was critical, and John had spent two years preparing his men for this one single task. They had trained in southern England in fair weather and foul, in rain and mud, for days on end without sleep and with full gear in the dark of night. Each man learned how to use everyone else's equipment and perform each other's duties in order to complete any task that they might have to cover for. There was not a single contingency that was not studied and practiced to perfection, no matter how small or insignificant.

Howard required two things of his men: that they had the capacity to think quickly, and that they would be the most physically fit men on earth. Each day, the men would be up before dawn on a five-mile cross country run. Breakfast would be at 7:00 a.m., then strenuous training for the day. Twice a month, the men were expected to complete a twenty-two-mile march in full pack with light machine guns called Brens that weighed twenty-three pounds and ND mortars and do it all in under five and a half hours. All the training was with live ammunition. The Germans hated fighting in the dark, and Company D had to take them totally by surprise. Because the assault would be at night, the training in the end would take place through the night. Starting at 8:00 p.m., the men would go on their daily five-mile cross country run, followed by dinner and then twelve hours of drills and field exercises. After a meal at 10 a.m. the next morning, they would hit the athletic field, and by 1:00 p.m. they would be sleeping, only to be awakened again at 8:00 p.m. to start all over again.

The weapons each man had to master were the Sten Carbine, the Enfield .303 rifle, the Bren machine gun, 2- and 3-inch mortars, and the Piat, an anti-tank projector. The Sten was a 9-mm submachine gun that could also be a single shot. It was not a very good rifle, often jamming, and occasionally firing on its own, but it was cheap to manufacture. The positive side is that it weighed only seven pounds and was accurate in close combat, when it worked.

At eight minutes past midnight, Howard's men were at their target. Their objective was not simple. Pegasus Bridge was a large steel structure. It had a water tower on the east side. Just north of the bridge was a machine gun pill box. An anti-tank emplacement was across the road, and an antiaircraft gun had arrived. There were fifty men assigned duty at the bridge, and tunnels had been built to connect the manned posts with the underground bunkers. The entire compound was surrounded by barbed wire, and the Germans were in the process of erecting large tall wooden poles around the bridge to deter any enemy planes from landing.

"As the Horsa's approached their targets Major Howard instructed the pilot Wallwork that he wanted him to break through the barbed wire with the nose of the plane. Wallwork thought to himself that there was not a chance in hell that he could land that big, heavy, cumbersome, badly overloaded, powerless Horsa with such precision, at midnight, over a bumpy and untested landing strip he could barely see. but out loud he assured Howard he would do his best. "

Stephen Ambrose,
Pegasus Bridge

The landing window was short, so a parachute was deployed to slow the glider down. "As the wheels touched ground, Wallwork yelled to Ainsworth, 'Stream!' Answorth pushed the button. The chute billowed out, 'and by golly it lifted the tail and shoved the nose wheel down.' The whole glider then bounced back up into the air, all three wheels now torn off. 'But the chute drew us back, and knocked the speed down tremendously, so in two seconds or less I told Ainsworth, 'Jettison!' So, Ainsworth pressed the tit and away went the parachutes and we were only going along possibly at sixty miles an hour. The Horsa hit the ground again, this time on its

skids.... "There was the most hellish din imaginable....
The nose had buried into the barbed wire, and crumbled.
The crash sent Wallwork (the pilot) and Ainsworth (the
co-pilot) flying forward still strapped in their seats, which
had broken loose. They went right out the cockpit and
onto the ground beneath. They were thus the first allied
troops to touch French soil on D-day. Both were, however,
unconscious. Inside the glider the troops, the sappers,
and company commander were also unconscious.'"

Stephen Ambrose,
Pegasus Bridge

When the men regained consciousness, they were able to
cut themselves loose, exit the plane, and achieve their objective
with complete surprise. To their credit, they captured both bridges
before they could be destroyed.

With perfect preparation, came powerful results and stunning
success. Attention to the smallest of details was the overriding
principle in accomplishing what to many seemed impossible but
was nonetheless achieved.

CHAPTER 9

"JUST GET BACK UP, ONE MORE TIME"

Tenacity / Endurance

"Opportunity is missed by most people because it is dressed in overalls and looks like work."

Thomas Edison

DAD HAD HIS SHARE of failures in his life, and as a teenager with some of the insecurities that came with that, I often felt that I may have been one of them. As I grew older, I realized he never, ever felt that way. Instead, he never stopped encouraging me to be better. I had misunderstood that encouragement as a sign of his disappointment in me.

He would constantly teach me that life is a process in which the experiences of everyday occurrences mold and shape us into who we are. He would say, "It all depends on how we choose to act or react to those challenges. They can become an opportunity for real growth to help us soar, or a stumbling block to bring us down. We are ultimately the ones who decide in which direction we will be pulled."

In my effort to belong, I explored the options available to me in a high school setting.

Becoming a school officer was a no because I was shy, and I definitely wasn't popular. Chess Club was a definite no, because I wasn't smart enough. So, joining the track team seemed like a natural fit. I loved to run. I was not good, especially at long distances, but I was fair at short sprints. So, I decided to run the hurdles, the 110 highs and the 180 lows (now referred to as the 100-meter highs and 140-meter lows). My second year as a junior, I knew I could do better, so I started to train in November for the track season the following spring. In early December, I broke my leg, and as a result, I was not able to continue my conditioning again until early February. In hopes of catching up with the rest of the team, my coach suggested I train with the distance runners. Distance runners belong to a unique fraternity that most people will never understand, and a majority would have no desire to become a part of. Almost all people stop when their bodies start to hurt, but to distance runners, pain is a mere motivation. I think they believe that the best way to make pain disappear is to chase it away by running farther and faster. After weeks of abuse, the coach decided to see if I had developed a new set of skills. So, in one of our first track meets of the spring season, he placed me in what was called the medley relay. It consisted of four runners. The first and second man would each run a 220-yard sprint, the third would run a 440 and the final runner completed the race with an 880. I was to anchor the race by running that 880. I soon discovered that running a half mile is a far cry from a 110- or 180-yard sprint over hurdles. By the time I received the baton on the last leg of the race, our team was in third place. As I flew down the track, the thought came to mind, "How hard could this be? It's the same as running seven high hurdle races back-to-back. I did that all the time in training."

I was elated to see that after one lap I had moved into first place. It was then that reality hit. And when it did, it was not kind.

As I came around the back stretch, I had increased our lead to over one hundred feet. I saw the coach yelling from the top of his lungs, and I was feeling so good, knowing how proud the coach must be of my incredible performance. Little did I realize that he was not yelling because of my stellar time but instead conveying to me what a total idiot I was. I had failed to pace myself. I had no idea how significant that would be until the start of the second lap. My desire was intense, but my body was not. It didn't matter what I wanted my muscles to do, they simply would not respond. Every muscle went out on strike, and by the end of the race I was in last place, and not by a small margin. My efforts to belong and develop meaningful relationships took a serious hit that day. The only consolation that was to come out of my pathetic performance was the fact that when I got home that night totally devastated, I was met with my father's ever-persistent optimism. "Well, son," he said. "At least you finished the race."

Years later, I memorized a poem that is a constant reminder that achieving great accomplishment in life is not a single event, but a long process of enduring and never giving up.

Good Timber

The tree that never had to fight,
For sun and sky and air and light,
But stood out in the open plain
And always got its share of rain,
Never became a forest king,
But lived and died a scrubby thing.

The man who never had to toil,
To gain and farm his patch of soil,
Who never had to win his share,
Of sun and sky and light and air
Never became a manly man,
But lived and died as he began.

Good timber does not grow with ease.
The stronger wind, the stronger trees.
The further sky, the greater length.
The more the storm, the more the strength.
By sun and cold, by rain and snow.
In trees and men good timbers grow.

Where thickest lies the forest growth,
We find the patriarchs of both,
And they hold council with the stars,
Whose broken branches show the scars
Of many winds and much of strife —
This is the common law of life.

Douglas Malloch

Thomas Edison exhibited the trait of "getting up one more time" about as well as anyone. That is why I have included him in this chapter.

Historical

Thomas Edison — One of the most prolific inventors of all time, from the light bulb to the phonograph

It was just another uneventful December evening. The snow was lightly falling, and the sun had just disappeared behind the western horizon. The country had not yet entered World War I. The year was 1914. Thomas Edison was busy with his latest inventions when a fire started in one of his buildings on his vast thirty-acre compound located at West Orange, New Jersey. It was 5:25 p.m. The fire was triggered by a highly combustible nitrate film in the film inspection building, which was a one-story wooden building. It then quickly spread to a nearby shed filled with lumber. Next came two tanks filled with alcohol, along with an adjoining five-story building containing phonograph recording cylinders and twenty tons of highly volatile phenol. The heat produced from this chemical was so intense that the concrete in the building basically melted. The fire continued with an unquenchable fury. It destroyed a carpenter shop containing rare hardwoods and a building used for shipping, followed by a printing building. The uncontrolled flames then destroyed the building holding the phonograph division. The loss of this particular building was catastrophic.

"Among the crowd of twelve thousand townspeople who flocked to watch on the valley slope overlooking the plant was Edison. He was strangely calm, even cheerful, after seeing that his laboratory was safe. 'Get mother and all her friends,' he said to Charles, his 24-year-old son. 'They'll never see a fire like this again.' When Charles objected, Edison said, 'It's all right. We've just got rid of a lot of rubbish.'"

The fire was finally out just after midnight, having consumed thirteen buildings and more than half of the complex. "'Mr. Edison, this is an awful catastrophe for you,' an executive from the advertising department said in a shaking voice. 'Yes, Mr. Maxwell, a big fortune has gone up in flames tonight, but isn't it a beautiful sight?' When daylight came, he penciled a brief statement to reporters. 'Am pretty well burned out, but tomorrow there will be some rapid mobilizing when I find out where I'm at.' Then he stretched out on a bench, rolled his coat into a pillow, and went to sleep".

Edmund Morris,
Edison

An article in *The New York Times* reported Edison's response: "I am sixty-seven years old. I'll start over again tomorrow."

The next day, found Edison with all of his employees busy at work cleaning up. No one lost their job and although his losses were devastating, he would soon rebuild. The next year of 1915 would find him $10 million in the black.

Edison exhibited the traits of most successful people. Rather than wallowing in self-pity, anger, resentment and the attitude of "Why me?" he simply decided to take control of his circumstances and be the master of his destiny and fate. He accepted what had just happened, put a smile on his face, rolled up his sleeves and went to work. He always loved what he was doing and took the bad with the good. We must find joy in our life's pursuits, regardless of what may be thrown in our way, if we are to do great things.

I believe that even though Thomas Edison during his lifetime had 1,093 patents, including the incandescent light bulb, the earliest motion picture camera, and the alkaline storage battery, his most amazing feat was the phonograph — especially considering the fact that he was totally deaf in one ear and hard of hearing in the other. In his lab at his summer residence in Fort Myers, Florida there is a phonograph with teeth marks on its base. He believed that if he put his teeth on the frame, he could feel the music's vibrations. As his very limited hearing worsened, he would place one end of a stick between his teeth and the other end against the speakers. He felt that he could then actually hear better than with the ear. He would eventually register over 240 inventions that were all based on sound.

The light bulb, the phonograph, motion pictures. His accomplishments were many, his failures myriad. His time was not spent lamenting his failures. He learned from his efforts which did not produce the desired results and used them as a platform upon which to build.

CHAPTER 10

"DON'T GET IN A PISSING CONTEST WITH A SKUNK"

Wisdom / Restraint

"Never wrestle with a pig. You both get dirty, and the pig likes it."

Mark Twain, 1872

I WAS ANGRY. NO, I had moved far beyond angry to livid. And what I sought was not justice. I wanted revenge. I am surprised at just how much time I had spent considering ways to extract it. Confronting my friend face to face would probably lead to a physical altercation, but the injustice he had perpetrated on me could not be ignored. My solution finally dawned on me. I could write him a letter. In it, I could carefully craft all the hurtful things I had endured. I could also guarantee that all the penetrating one-liners I usually thought of after the fact would not be lost, and a letter would be permanent. To get rid of it, he would have to put forth a little more effort than is required today. Instead of hitting the delete button, he would actually have to take the time to throw it away. My hope was that he would read it over and over again and finally realize the hurt and pain he had caused me, and I would win. Or at least I thought I would.

I took several days to craft this missive, and upon completion, I gave it to my father to proofread. After he had perused the letter, he turned to me and said, "You have some strong feelings here, son. But if you think this letter will send your friend into a cowering retreat, or bring him into total surrender, agreeing with everything you have written, then you're sadly mistaken." "And why is that?" I asked. "Because unless he is open to what you are saying, and he sees that he has a need to change, his attitude will remain more resolute than before. He will send you a stronger response, and you'll fire back with an even more terse note, and the battle will only escalate. I suggest you take the letter and put it in your desk drawer and leave it there for a week or two. After you have had a chance to cool down and put things in their proper perspective, you might feel differently. If not, then send the letter. But be forewarned that once this battle is waged, the only ending will be when you finally walk away because you can't stand the smell."

Hence my first lesson: Don't get in a pissing contest with a skunk; you'll just come out stinking.

In the end, the letter was never sent. I allowed my feelings toward him to soften, and oddly enough, we are still friends.

Historical

Mark Twain — A colorful and beloved American author

Mark Twain once said, "Never argue with stupid people. They will drag you down to their level and then beat you with experience."

Samuel Clemens, a.k.a. Mark Twain, was born in 1835. During his life, he was a riverboat pilot, gold miner, journalist, lecturer, humorist, publisher, and inventor. But most notably, he was one of America's greatest authors.

As a young boy living in the small town of Hannibal, Missouri on the bank of the Mississippi River, there were few people in the world who had ever heard of him. As an adult living in Hartford, Connecticut, there were few people in the world who had not heard of him. He came from a family of meager means to become one of the wealthiest men in America.

He met Olivia Langdon in 1867 and was immediately smitten. After a short two-week courtship, he proposed, and she said no. He was not deterred, and over the next several years he wrote close to 200 letters to her. In February of 1870, she finally gave in, and they were married. Olivia was a beautiful young lady. She was petite, calm, refined and well cultured and very religious. Mark Twain, on the other hand, exhibited none of these attributes. One day, Twain cut himself shaving and let out a whole string of swear words. His wife, in an effort to show him just how offensive he had just been, repeated his profanities right back to him, to which he replied, "You have the words, dear, but you don't know the tune."

At times He was extremely creative. An advertising poster for his first public lecture in San Francisco read:

Mark Twain (Honolulu correspondent of the Sacramento Union) will deliver a lecture on the Sandwich Islands on Tuesday evening, October 2.

A SPLENDID ORCHESTRA is in town but has not been engaged.

A DEN OF FEROCIOUS WILD BEASTS will be on exhibition in the next block. MAGNIFICENT FIREWORKS were in contemplation for this occasion, but the idea has been abandoned.

A GRAND TORCHLIGHT PROCESSION may be expected. In fact, the public are privileged to expect whatever they please.

Doors open at 7 o'clock.

The lecture was sold out, as was every lecture he delivered in future years.

Mark Twain was also a wonderful study in contrast.

He was extremely rich,

Many books and lectures made him one of the wealthiest authors of the nineteenth century,

He was also extremely poor

His business sense was so poor he ended up totally bankrupt. He turned down an offer to invest in the telephone because he felt there was no market for such an invention. However, he turned around and put most of his wealth into an automatic compositor, which was a machine with 18,000 moving parts that was to replace the efforts of six men in setting type for printing. The machine was never viable, and Mark Twain lost all of his wealth in this ill-advised venture.

He was opinionated

Twain usually said what he thought. Speaking of Congress, he once said, "Suppose you were an idiot, and suppose you were a member of Congress. But I repeat myself." He also said, "All congresses and parliaments have a kindly feeling for idiots, and a compassion for them, on account of personal experience and heredity."

He was constrained

Mark Twain had many opinions and was a prodigious letter writer. His wife was a calming influence in his life and convinced him on many occasions to take his scathing correspondence and place it in a drawer of his desk to allow him time to cool down. As a result, many of these letters were never sent.

In an article in *The New York Post* on March 22, 2014, Maria Konnikova wrote, "Whenever Abraham Lincoln felt the urge to tell someone off, he would compose what he called a hot letter. He'd pile all of his anger into a note, then put it aside until his emotions cooled down." Dorris Kearns Goodwin once explained, "He would then write 'never sent never signed' on it."

> "Among public figures who need to think twice about their choice of words, the unsent angry letter has a venerable tradition. Its purpose is twofold. It serves as a type of emotional catharsis — a way to let it all out without the repercussions of true engagement. And it acts as a strategic catharsis, an exercise in saying what you really think, which Mark Twain (himself a notable non-sender of correspondence) believe provided 'unallowable frankness and freedom.' "
>
> Maria Konnikova

Mark Twain's Notable Quotes

"Be good and you will be lonesome."

"Let us endeavor so to live that when we come to die, even the undertaker will be sorry."

"To succeed in business, avoid my example."

"Never put off 'til tomorrow what may be done day after tomorrow just as well."

"The man with a new idea is a crank until the idea succeeds."

"Always do right. This will gratify some and astonish the rest."

"When in doubt, tell the truth."

CHAPTER 11

"HAVE A HAP, HAP, HAPPY DAY"

Joy /
Happiness

"Life is like an old-time rail journey. Delays, sidetracks, smoke, dust, cinders, and jolts interspersed only occasionally by beautiful vistas and thrilling burst of speed. The trick is to thank the Lord for letting you have the ride."

Jenkins Lloyd Jones

I HAD A CONVERSATION WITH my father just months before he passed away. Two questions I asked of him were, first, "Tell me what you think it will be like in heaven?" After not receiving any insightful answers. I then asked if he felt there would be golf in heaven (He loved golf). I loved his response. "Well, son, if there isn't golf, it is only because they have come up with a game that is a lot more fun." The second question I asked was, "If you had to live your life over, what would you change?" This answer bothered me for quite some time. "Son, I would not change a thing." I felt he was serious, and as I thought back on my own life, I realized there were a lot of things I would do differently. One day it finally occurred to me what he really meant. Sure, there were a lot of day-to-day decisions he would probably change. But the general direction or course he chose for his life is what he really loved and was passionate about.

I have sweet childhood memories, and many were made rich through music. Every day started out with dad leading the family in a song called, *It's a Hap, Hap, Happy Day*, and every day ended with him giving us 'Josepher Rides' to bed.

I remember the following from when I was young:

TVs were black and white with poor reception, and the programing was limited. We couldn't afford to go to the movies too often, and when we did, we knew the movie was over when the words "THE END" appeared on the screen not ten minutes later after the credits have finally finished. Disneyland was a new theme park, but it was a day's travel away and we could only afford to visit there about every four or five years. Music came on AM FM radios with limited reception. And so, by default, LP vinyl records or 45s became our primary source of entertainment. These records resonated back then with the same clarity they do today. It's fun to see their popularity return.

The LPs we would listen to again and again were mainly musicals, *My Fair Lady*, *The Music Man*, *Carousel*, and *Oklahoma*. The music my kids listen to is pop, rap, hip-hop, jazz, and just about anything that is loud.

Dad made sure that music was important in the lives of all his kids, so it just naturally followed that as each of us turned six, we were required to learn a musical instrument. I really had no interest in learning to play anything musical. What I really wanted to play was football and basketball and anything else ending in "ball." When I asked the go-to question of "Why do I have to?" I was answered with the go-to response: "Because I said so." So, I resigned myself to make the best of the situation. My older brother had picked the trumpet, and my older sister settled on the violin, so when my turn came, I told my father I wanted to play the drums. Dad quickly informed me that the drums were not a musical instrument. I argued that if they weren't, then why were they in bands? I don't remember what his response was. But the answer was still no. So, I settled on the clarinet. When I became a parent, I realized why Dad had said no to the drums. A house full of kids produces a decibel level high enough on its own without the addition of the constant pounding of drums.

Dad had many gifts and talents. He loved music, but singing was a talent he did not possess. He was loud and enthusiastic, but terribly off-key. To his credit, he did know the lyrics to all the contemporary tunes of his day, and the rest really didn't matter. Every morning as we started the day, Dad would get us out of bed early and lead us in a song, The same song, every single morning. The tune was upbeat and rather rousing, and the lyrics went as follows:

It's a hap, hap, happy day,
toodle-oodle-oodle-oodle-oodle-lay!
For you and me, for us and we,
all the clouds have rolled away!
It's a hap, hap, happy day,
toodle-oodle-oodle-oodle-oodle-lay!
The sun shines bright and the world's so bright,
it's a hap, hap, happy day!

As a child growing up, I always thought Dad had made up his own lyrics to this song, and I thought it was a little on the corny side. But Dad wasn't afraid of what others thought, and a goofy song would be the last thing to stop him. Corny or not, the results were infectious, spreading to every member of the family. We left the house with a smile on our face and a little more speed to our cadence, more skip to our step. At least the day started out on an upbeat, positive note.

Historical

1 song on the British BBC Radio during the Battle of Britain in World War II

Just recently, I started to do a little research to see if there really was such a song, and to my surprise there was. I wished Dad had shared a little background to the song, because it would have carried much greater significance. The lyrics were written in 1939 by Sammy Timberg and Winston Sharpies for the animated feature film, *Gulliver's Travels*. The song became a huge hit, especially in Great Britain in 1940. It was played frequently on the BBC Radio Network. Its popularity coincided with the darkest days for Great Britain in World War II, from August throughout September of that year.

The British were being bombed day and night by Hitler's Luftwaffe in what became known as the Battle of Britain. Hitler had unleashed his terrible war machine against the population centers in England in an attempt to destroy the morale of the Brits. England stood alone as the only country in the world fighting the Axis power. The U.S. would not enter the war until December 8, 1941, the day following the attack on Pearl Harbor.

I find it amazing that when the British people were living in constant worry and fear, not knowing when the next bombs would be falling, that the most popular song on the radio was about having a "hap, hap, happy day."

During these dark days, The Prime Minister of Great Britain was Winston Churchill. He gave many speeches, including his famous Battle of Britain speech delivered to Parliament on June 18, 1940, just prior to the start of that battle.

"I would say to the house as I said to those who have joined this government: 'I have nothing to offer but blood, toil, tears, and sweat. We have before us an ordeal of the most grievous kind. We have before us many, many long months of struggle and of suffering. You ask what is our policy? I will say it is to wage war by sea, land, and air, with all our might and with all the strength that God can give us: To wage war against a monstrous tyranny, never surpassed in the dark lamentable catalogue of human crime. That is our policy. You ask what is our aim? I can answer with one word: victory, victory at all costs. We shall not flag nor fail. Let us therefore brave ourselves to our duties and so bear ourselves that if the British Empire and its commonwealth last for a thousand years, men will say, this was their finest hour."

The ability to smile in the face of adversity is a wonderful trait to cultivate. In the dark days of the Civil War, President Lincoln shared a humorous story with his Cabinet. After the meeting, one of his Cabinet members scolded the President for his levity, saying, "Mr. President, with the country in such dire circumstances, I feel it totally inappropriate to tell such a story." President Lincoln then said, "Gentlemen, if I did not laugh, I should die, and you need this medicine as much as I."

CHAPTER 12

"IT'S EASIER TO GAIN FORGIVENESS THAN PERMISSION"

Initiative

"'Thou shalt not' is soon forgotten, but 'once upon a time' lasts forever."

Philip Pullman

ERIC, MY YOUNGEST SON, came home one day with an old, rusted bird cage. He was excited because now he had a home for his parakeet. When I reminded him that he didn't have a parakeet, he immediately informed me that this was not a problem. He was going to earn some money so he could go buy one. I quickly put an end to this line of thinking by informing Eric that we were not going to get a parakeet, regardless of who was paying.

"Why can't I get a parakeet, Dad?" he asked. "Because I said so," was my answer. "Why not, Dad?" he asked a second time. "Because I said so." A third time came the same question, quickly followed by the same answer. When I finally realized that this was going to be a long afternoon, I changed my approach.

"Parakeets are noisy, they make a mess, they have to be constantly fed, and they go through a lot of newspaper." When I finished, I was met with a rather startling response. After appearing to be in deep thought, Eric's simple reply was, "Okay, Dad." And with a smile on his face, he skipped out of the room. "That was way too easy," I thought. But I was happy to have put the whole matter to bed.

Three weeks later, it was my birthday. It was a rather normal day, except for the unusual excitement from my youngest son. He could hardly contain himself. That night we celebrated with cake and ice cream, and a few gifts. Eric's present was an envelope with a small card inside that read: "Dad, your birthday present is in the garage. Love, Eric." When I went out to see what it could possibly be, there on the work bench sat Eric's old beat-up secondhand bird cage with — you guessed it — a bright green parakeet inside. Since he could not get permission to get a parakeet, he knew he could gain forgiveness by obtaining the bird through a gift he knew I could not return. By the way, he was very committed to that bird and took great care of it.

This was without question my favorite "ism." Dad's intentions in teaching this valuable principle to his young son were simply this: there are many noble tasks that we can be engaged in, if we act quickly without delay. Quite often, I would hear Dad say, "Take the bull by the horns" or "Remember, son, he who hesitates loses." I observed Dad applying this philosophy in his own life on more than one occasion. The caveat in teaching me this lesson was that there were three rules that had to be followed:

1. Whatever I did, it had to be a noble act
2. It had to be morally right
3. It had to benefit mankind.

The one thing Dad failed to take into account was the simple mind of a young boy. I thought all of my actions were noble and morally right, and I also believed that they would benefit at least one member of the human race: myself.

When I was a sophomore in high school, my father was offered the job to be principal of my school. This created some interesting challenges, and also some unique opportunities for a young boy. Two advantages for me were that many of my teachers were afraid to fail the principal's son, so I probably received a fair number of passing grades that I really didn't deserve. It also gave me a free pass to come and go to the principal's office any time I wanted to, even if he was not there. One day, while visiting his office I had one of those moments of pure revelation. On the shelf right in front of me were all the forms the office typically used for hall passes. They read: "Please admit (Brent) to class late, please send (Brent) to the office immediately." And so on.

My father and I had basically the same name. His name was John Larsen and mine was Brent John Larsen. I would fill out the forms and sign them using only my middle and last name, John Larsen. I quickly developed a reasonable likeness to his signature, and so for three years, with the help of friends bringing these notes into class, I was able to avoid tests that I had not prepared for. Better yet, I could get some of my friends out of class, and we would go up to Bonneville Golf Course for nine holes in the middle of the day. I thought I had been so clever, until three days before my class was to graduate, Dad came home with 740 graduation certificates. He handed them to me and said, "I just received these today, and there is no way I am going to be able to sign them all. So here, son, get started." I looked at him with one of those "I have no idea what you're talking about" expressions on my face. His immediate response was, "Don't give me that innocent look. I have watched my signature written by you come through the office for the past three years, and you have got me down pretty darn good. So, get started." When I asked why he had never said anything, his response was a sign of how much he really understood me. He said, "Son, I know being the principal's kid was not easy, and so I felt there were certain things I would just let ride. I was aware of the tests you missed, and even of the golf games played, and I was willing to let it go as long as it didn't get out of hand." Oh, how I loved him for allowing me to learn from my own mistakes. I ended up signing most of the graduation certificates that year, and I have often wondered if that forged signature made those certificates invalid.

Historical

Teddy Roosevelt — 26th U.S. President, reformer, conservationist, and dynamic leader

He lived in the White House and was the youngest of six kids. His name was Quentin Roosevelt. His father was the youngest president to ever serve, and his name was Teddy. Young Quentin and his father shared a lot in common. Both were extremely active physically as well as intellectually. Teddy loved the "strenuous life" and Quentin lived it. They both did everything in life with incredible enthusiasm and were not afraid to try almost anything. Fear of failure or fear of what others thought never crossed their minds.

Quentin was the very essence of "better to ask forgiveness than permission."

Both Teddy and Quentin attended Harvard. They loved their country. Teddy fought in the Spanish-American War in 1898 and came back a national hero. Quentin fought in World War I and never came back. As a fighter pilot, his plane was shot down over France in 1918. He is buried in Normandy alongside his older brother Teddy, Jr., who died in World War II. Teddy Roosevelt took the death of his youngest son very hard and died himself six months later of a coronary embolism. He was sixty years old.

I learned from the example of my father, and Quentin definitely learned from his.

Teddy Roosevelt was a man of decisive action, and he did not waste a lot of time asking permission from others to do what he felt needed to be done. By signing into law the Antiquities Act on June 8, 1906, Roosevelt was given the perfect tool to match his personality: the authority to act on his own, unobstructed by

Congress. The act gave him the power to provide federal protection for cultural and natural resources of historic or scientific interest on federal land. The most famous was establishing the Grand Canyon as a national monument in 1908. It was later changed to a national park in 1919. When he established the monument, he said, "In the Grand Canyon, Arizona has a natural wonder which is in kind absolutely unparalleled throughout the rest of the world. Leave it as it is. You cannot improve on it. The ages have been at work on it, and man can only mar it."

Roosevelt loved the rugged outdoor life and was an avid hunter. Yet at the same time, he was a champion of conservation efforts. As President, he was the force behind establishing:

> 5 National Parks
> 18 National Monuments
> 4 National Game Reserves
> 51 Federal Bird Sanctuaries

He created the U.S. Forest Service in 1905, and established 230 million acres of public lands, which included 150 national forests

His list of other accomplishments is impressive by any standard.

Age 22   Harvard graduate magna cum laude

    23   Elected to New York state assembly (youngest to ever serve)

    24   Published first major literary work, "The Naval War of 1812" (becomes required reading at Annapolis Naval Academy) Commissioned as Second Lieutenant in the national guard Elected speaker of Republican Assembly New York

    26   Establishes Elkhorn Cattle Ranch in North Dakota

    29   Establishes Boone and Crockett club, The nation's first fair-hunting organization

31   Starts as U.S. Civil Service Commissioner in Washington D.C.

37   Police Commissioner of New York City

39   Appointed Assistant Secretary of the Navy

40   Organizes the Rough Riders to fight in the Spanish American War
Elected Governor of New York

42   Becomes Vice President of the United States
Becomes President following the assassination of President McKinley

48   Awarded the Nobel Peace Prize

51   Spends a year on an African safari

54   Nominated as presidential candidate for the Progressive Party
Survives assassination attempt in Wisconsin

56   Spends four months charting an unexplored tributary of the Amazon

60   Dies at Sagamore Hill on Oyster Bay in New York

Wrote 38 books:

2 volumes on "The Naval War of 1812"

4 volumes on "Winning of the West"

23 volumes on topics of history, natural history, biographies, political philosophy

He would end up writing over 50,000 personal letters

He read a minimum of one book a day

His often-quoted proverb was, "Speak softly and carry a big stick."

Edith Roosevelt called her youngest son Quentin "a fine bad little boy." While living in the White House, young Quentin had organized a group of friends into what became known as the "White House Gang," operating out of the attic of the White House. Their exploits were well known by the Secret Service since they were often the target of attacks from the "Gang." During the winter months, the security details were often dodging snowballs being thrown from the roof of the White House. The Secret Service failed to thwart Quentin's covert operation of sneaking a pony up the elevator to the second floor of the White House (to cheer up his sick brother, Archie), and shooting presidential portraits in the halls with spitballs. They were also ineffective in stopping the gang from carving a baseball diamond into the white house lawn.

The Gang's most memorable activity came during their famous "battle for the flag." The Gang had divided up into two armies: one led by Taffy (William Taft's son) and the other by Q (Quentin). A victory flag would be awarded to the army who could hold the high ground for at least three minutes. Taffy had gained the advantage by securing a water hose which he used to successfully repel any advance by Q. The tide of the war quickly changed when Taffy's water hose suddenly went dry. Why? Because Q had secured an ax, and had chopped the hose to pieces.

The President had witnessed the unfolding of the events from his office window, and immediately came storming out with the following dialogue taking place:

"TR (panting heavily): Too late! Too late, by George! Quentin — I mean, George Washington — come here with your i-n-c-r-i-m-i-n-a-t-i-n-g hatchet! In the heat of battle, many acts, which would not be c-o-u-n-t-e-n-a-n-c-e-d at other times, may be excusable, or at least subject to sympathetic interpretation, of course. You understand that boys?

Q: Sure. You mean that's the reason why I did it? I did it because something had to be done immediately.

TR: That's e-x-a-c-t-l-y it! The point is always to do *something* quickly. Because if you don't, the other fellow will. You may be wrong — you were here — but you have, at least i-n-i-t-i-a-t-e-d action. When the action is wrong, you must admit it and correct it by some further action.

Q (looking at the severed hose): I don't see how *this* can be corrected.

TR: Only by an entirely new garden hose. It was government property. Still is, but also, no longer. You cannot imagine the difficulties involved, and the things required to be done, in order to replace it. It will even cost money, part of that which I am earning — or was earning, when interrupted by a dispatch regarding the progress of this war and left hurriedly for the field.

Q: Well, of course you're right; but we've learned our lesson, you know.

TR: We? Don't you mean yourself? And what have you learned?

Q: Not to cut up garden hoses.

TR: And not to use fire axes on anything but a fire.

Q (with a touch of wistfulness): We're not so likely to have a fire.

TR: Not with all this water around! You escape, Quentin, only because of the extenuating circumstances arising out of the heat of battle.

With that, he turned on his heels and marched back to the Executive Office."

Edmund Morris,
Theodore Rex,

Roosevelt Side Notes

'Dee-lighted!' was Roosevelt's sincere greeting to a new acquaintance, often with a huge grin and energetic handshake. His impressions on others were often profound.

"A statesman from England said, 'Do you know the two most wonderful things I have seen in your country? Niagara Falls and the President of the United States, both great wonders of nature. Their common quality which photographers and paintings fail to capture is a perpetual flow of torrential energy, a sense of motion even to stillness. Both are physically thrilling to be near.'

'You go to the White House,' wrote Richard Washburn Child. 'You shake hands with Roosevelt and hear him talk—and then go home to wring the personality out of your clothes.'

Describing their father, one of his children humorously put it, 'He was 'The bride at every wedding, and the corpse at every funeral.'"

Edmund Morris,
The Rise of Theodore Roosevelt

Just prior to giving a speech in Milwaukee, Wisconsin on October 14, 1912, he was shot in an assassination attempt with a Colt revolver by a 36-year-old New York unemployed saloonkeeper. Roosevelt was fifty-three. The bullet penetrated his steel eyeglass case and then went through his fifty-page speech he had carried in his coat pocket before lodging in his chest. He refused any medical help until after he had delivered his speech. "Friends, I shall ask you to be as quiet as possible. Ladies and gentlemen, I don't know whether you fully understand that I have just been shot, but it takes more than that to kill a bull moose." Ninety minutes later, with his breathing shortened and his voice becoming weaker, he finally allowed his security detail to take him to the hospital. It was deemed too dangerous to remove the bullet and so he carried it in his chest for the rest of his life.

CHAPTER 13

"THE SHEEP GROW FAT ONLY UNDER THE SHEPHERD'S EYE"

Vision

"There is an old Wayne Gretzky quote that I love: 'I skate to where the puck is going to be, not where it has been.' And we've always tried to do that at Apple. Since the very, very beginning, and we always will."

Steve Jobs

PART 1 A Hands-on CEO

AS A YOUNG BOY, this saying had a rather simple and defined meaning: "If you want to succeed in life, then it will require two things:

1. Your undivided personal attention
2. A lot of enthusiasm for the task at hand (Is your heart really in it?)

Nothing great was ever accomplished without these two ingredients.

My first foray into the world of cars was when I learned about the National Soap Box Derby Race that was held each year in Denton, Ohio. I didn't necessarily want to go back to Ohio, but the vision of building my own car was intoxicating to a young ten-year-old boy. The freedom to drive anywhere I wanted to go (as long as I could enlist enough friends to push) was an incredible thought. Not far from our home was a rather large, long steep hill that was ideal for racing down. Many of my carefree summer days were spent searching for the perfect wheels for our cart. Most lawn mower wheels were too small, and bike wheels were too big. Wheelbarrow tires were just about right. Our first cart was rather simple, like my Pinewood Derby car, but with a significant difference: the cart tires stayed on. The cart was basically built by running a two-by-twelve board down the center approximately six feet long, with two permanently nailed two-by-fours attached perpendicularly on the front and back. These would then become our axles. On our first test drive we quickly realized we had a huge flaw in our engineering when we drifted off the road through Mrs. Evans' rose garden. With the front axle permanently nailed on the front, it was rather hard to steer. Actually, it was impossible. Two thoughts raced through my mind just before impact. The first was that this collision was going to hurt, and the second was how mad Mrs. Evans was going to be at seeing her destroyed roses. It was an expensive lesson to learn. Rose bushes were not cheap. Our new design proved to be much better and would save us a lot of money in accumulated damages. We replaced the nails on the front axle with a large bolt and nut which allowed the two-by-four to rotate freely. We would sit on the center board and put our feet on the front two-by-four axel and steer with our feet. It was a simple plan: push the right foot forward to turn left and the left foot forward to turn right. The next design we had to improve on was how to stop. We realized that dragging our feet had two problems. We were not only wearing out a lot of tennis shoes, but we were also sacrificing our ability to steer. Our feet needed to remain on the front axle. Our solution was to nail small boards to the side of the cart with a single nail so we could pull up on one end of the board, forcing the other end down into the road. Instead of going through a lot of tennis shoes, we were now going through a lot of boards. Our designs improved over the summer so that by August we had replaced steering with our feet to controlling the front axle with a rope and pulley system. The brakes now rubbed against the tires instead of the road. We also had built a small bed on the back of the cart to allow us to carry passengers. We knew we had finally arrived when we could take our cart to the top of the street, where a line of kids was waiting, each willing to pay ten cents for a ride down to the bottom of the hill. We thought we were going to be the richest kids ever.

All great endeavors in the world had individuals that exhibited both traits: enthusiasm and personal involvement. They simply were "all in." Just like Thomas Edison with the light bulb, Henry Ford with his cars, the Wright Brothers with their plane, and Steve Jobs with his computers, along with many others. In my own life, whether it was a science project with other students, a social activity like organizing a school dance, or a financial endeavor like creating my own lawn cutting business with my friends, if I was not there personally overseeing the whole thing, then the chances of success were greatly diminished. I learned years later that this approach was not all it was cracked up to be. Delegation (getting others to accept accountability and ownership) was also critical and greatly increased the chances of success.

The real lesson that Dad was trying to teach was that if we wanted to succeed — whether it be in our relations with others, our marriage, our community, our religion, or our work — we need to be there, to be actively involved, and to come with a high level of enthusiasm.

Without even realizing it, with my new "transportation company," I was actually incorporating Dad's shepherd philosophy.

Historical

Steve Jobs — Visionary who created Apple Inc., one of the most successful companies ever

It all started with what was called a "blue box." It could generate the tones necessary to control the telephone network, allowing the user to make long-distance calls for free. It was illegal, but sales were good. Steve Wozniak was its creator, but Steve Jobs saw its potential. If it wasn't for Wozniak's blue box, according to Jobs, "There wouldn't have been an Apple." The year was 1971.

In March 1976, Steve Wozniak finished a basic computer that would become the Apple I. On April 1, 1976, Apple Computer Company was started in Steve's bedroom and later moved to the garage at his parent's home in Los Altos, California. A year later, they would introduce the Apple II, which became one of the most successful microcomputers in the world. By age twenty-five, Steve Jobs was worth over $250 million (roughly $800 million In today's market).

In 1985, Steve Jobs was forced to leave the company he had started. He and CEO John Scully, along with the board of directors, could not see eye to eye. Following his departure, he started NeXT, a company that specialized in computers for businesses and higher education, and in 1986, Pixar came into being. Its first 3D computer animated feature film was *Toy Story* followed by other such notables as *A Bug's Life, Monsters, Inc., Cars, Finding Nemo, WALL-E* and *Up*, to name a few. In 2005, Disney purchased Pixar with stock worth $7.4 billion, making Steve Jobs the largest Disney stockholder.

With the departure of Steve Jobs from Apple, the company would struggle for the next eleven years. In 1997, Apple acquired

NeXT and Steve eventually returned as CEO. He brought the company back from near bankruptcy and set it on a trajectory to become the most successful business in the world through innovations such as the iMac, iPod, iPad, iTunes, App Store (iOS) and — most famous of all — the iPhone. His name is on over 450 patents.

A comprehensive understanding of the how and why Apple became so successful can be found by examining the philosophy of Steve Jobs. A good example is contained in his commencement address delivered at Stanford University June 12, 2005.

"Today I want to tell you three stories from my life. That's it. No big deal. Just three stories.

The First Story is About Connecting the Dots...

Much of what I stumbled into by following my curiosity and intuition turned out to be priceless later on. Let me give you one example: Reed College at the time offered the best calligraphy instruction in the country. I decided to take a calligraphy class to learn how to do this. I learned about serif and sans serif typefaces, about varying the amount of space between different letter combinations, about what makes great typography great. It was beautiful, historical, artistically subtle in a way that science can't capture, and I found it fascinating.

None of this had even a hope of any practical application in my life. But ten years later, when we were designing the first Macintosh computer, it all came back to me, and we designed it all into the Mac. It was the first computer with beautiful typography. If I had never dropped in on that single course in college, the Mac would never had multiple typefaces or proportionally spaced fonts...

Again, you can't connect the dots looking forward; you can only connect them looking backward. So, you have to trust that the dots will somehow connect in your future. You have to trust in something — your gut, destiny, life, karma, whatever.

This approach has never let me down, and it has made all the difference in my life.

The Second Story is About Love and Loss

I was lucky — I found what I loved to do early in life. Woz and I started Apple in my parents' garage when I was twenty. We worked hard, and in ten years Apple had grown from just the two of us in a garage into a $2 billion company with over 4,000 employees. We had just released our finest creation — the Macintosh — a year earlier, and I had just turned thirty. And I got fired. How can you get fired from a company you started? Well, as Apple grew, we hired someone who I thought was very talented to run the company with me, and for the first year or so things went well. But then our vision of the future began to diverge and eventually we had a falling out. When we did, our Board of Directors sided with him. So, at thirty, I was out, and very publicly out. What had been the focus of my entire adult life was gone, and it was devastating.

I really didn't know what to do for a few months... I still loved what I did. The turn of events at Apple had not changed that one bit. I had been rejected, but I was still in love. And so, I decided to start over.

I didn't see it then, but it turned out that getting fired from Apple was the best thing that could have ever happened to me. The heaviness of being successful was replaced by the lightness of being a beginner again, less sure about everything. It freed me to enter one of the most creative periods of my life.

During the next five years, I started a company named NeXT, and another company named Pixar. Pixar went on to create the world's first computer animated feature film, *Toy Story*, and is now the most successful animated studio in the world. In a remarkable turn of events, Apple bought NeXT, I returned to Apple, and the technology we developed at NeXT is at the heart of Apple's current renaissance...

I'm pretty sure none of this would have happened if I hadn't been fired from Apple. It was awful tasting medicine, but I guess the patient needed it. Sometimes life hits you in the head with a brick, but don't lose faith. I'm convinced that the only thing that kept me going was that I loved what I did. The only way to be truly satisfied is to do what you believe is great work. And the only way to do great work is to love what you do. If you haven't found it yet, keep looking. Don't settle.

The Third Story Is About Death

When I was seventeen, I read a quote that went something like this: "If you live each day as if it was your last, someday you'll most certainly will be right." It made an impression on me, and since then, for the past 33 years, I have looked in the mirror every morning and asked myself, "If today were the last day of my life, would I want to do what I am about to do today?"

Remembering that I'll be dead soon is the most important tool I've ever encountered to help me make the big choices in life. Because almost everything — all external expectations, all pride, all fear of embarrassment or failure — these things just fall away in the face of death, leaving only what is truly important. Remembering that you are going to die is the best way I know to avoid the trap of thinking you have something to lose. There is no reason not to follow your heart...

Your time is limited so don't waste it living someone else's life... Don't let the noise of others' opinions drown out your own inner voice.

Footnote

"Jobs' prickly behavior was partly driven by his perfectionism, and his impatience with those who made compromises in order to get a product out on time and on budget. One day Jobs came into the cubicle of Larry Kenyon, an engineer who was working on the Macintosh operating system, and complained that it was taking too long to boot up. Kenyon started to explain, but Jobs cut him off. 'If it could save a person's life, would you find a way to shave ten seconds off the boot time?' he asked. Kenyon allowed that he probably could. Jobs went to a whiteboard and showed that if there were five million people using the Mac, and it took ten seconds extra to turn it on every day, that added up to three hundred million or so hours per year that people would save, which was the equivalent of at least one hundred lifetimes saved per year.

Larry was suitably impressed, and a few weeks later he came back and it booted up twenty-eight seconds faster," Atkinson recalled. "Steve had a way of motivating by looking at the bigger picture.

The result was that the Macintosh team came to share Jobs' passion for making a great product, not just a profitable one," said Hertzfeld. "The goal was never to beat the competition or make a lot of money. It was to do the greatest thing possible, or even a little greater."

Walter Isaacson,
Steve Jobs

Currently, Apple stands alone as the most successful company in the world with market capitalization of over $3 trillion dollars.

Steve died of complications from a pancreatic neuroendocrine tumor on October 5, 2011. He was fifty-six years old.

PART 2 A Shepherd of Sheep

A shepherd never told the sheep what or when to eat, he took them to where they could be fed. He simply provided the opportunity. A shepherd is always there and has compassion for his sheep.

Dad was a shepherd to many different kinds of sheep. First and foremost, he was a shepherd to his family. Under his stewardship, we were well fed, had a roof over our heads and were protected from harm and danger. Second, he was a shepherd to those who worked under him, under his charge. He ran a successful school district audio visual department and was a high school principal. His photography business was an outlier. Dad was also a very religious man. He spent endless hours of service every week seeing to the needs of members of his church, and his community.

He was what Carl Sandberg referred to as "velvet and steel." He could be fiercely intimidating with his deep booming voice that at times seemed to make the walls vibrate, and his large frame was always imposing. I often felt his penetrating blue eyes could see right through me, and with a vice-like handshake that could make the strongest hand wilt. These were all secondary to his huge bear hugs. They were smothering, but at the same time, kind and comforting. They gave a reassuring feeling that you were now very safe, and that nothing could hurt you. Long after Dad's passing, people who knew him would stop me on the street to tell me that the one thing they missed most about John Larsen was his big hugs. Dad could be very demanding one minute and the next minute so tender and kind.

One night I was riding in the car with Dad to run an errand to the store, and on the way back home, Dad asked if I would mind if he made a quick stop. We drove down a small rutted dirt road and pulled up in front of a small wooden frame home that had seen better days: the screen door had holes in it, the paint was peeling on the window seals, the drapes had faded from the relentless attack of the sun, and the shrubs and been given free reign for many years now, pretty much taking over the small gardens. It was late, but after several knocks on the door, an elderly man appeared. He looked like he was in his mid- to late-eighties, a slow shuffle to his step and a little hunched over. When the screen door swung open, the hunched-over figure suddenly straightened up a little, and with a smile that took over a worn face, reached out for that anticipated Big John hug. The elderly man, Joseph, had immigrated from

Sweden when he was young. He had lived a simple yet productive life. He had married and had a large family. His kids had all married and moved away, starting families of their own. He now lived alone; his wife having passed away years earlier. I watched as Dad gave Joseph a small envelope, talked for another few minutes, gave him another hug and left the dimly lit front porch as Joseph stood silently waving goodbye before he closed the door.

When Dad got back in the car, there were a few small tears escaping from his eyes. When I asked for an explanation of what I just witnessed, Dad's simple answer was, "Today was Joseph's birthday, and I just wanted to stop and give him a birthday card and wish him well." When I asked Dad why he was so tender about it all, his response was, "Joseph told me that not one single person had remembered his birthday, no family or neighbors or friends, but that he knew John Larsen would not forget him."

I later ran across a calendar where Dad, in his own handwriting, had checked off the birthdays of a fairly large group of people. I tallied them, and found that in 1967, Dad had quietly delivered 320 birthday cards. He had personally delivered each one. They were to neighbors and people who had been close to him. As the principal of a local high school, he gave those cards to his faculty and staff. This he always did with a little more fanfare than with the neighbors, family, and friends. First thing in the morning, he would go into the classroom of the teachers whose birthday it was. He would deliver the card in front of the entire class and lead them in a rousing rendition of the *Happy Birthday* song before leaving. When I asked Dad why he always followed this same little tradition of going into the classroom early in the day, he said with a sparkle in his eye, "If I go in at the start of first period, I find that throughout the day word soon gets around, calls are made to moms at home, and by the end of the day, cakes and decorations are arriving, and an ordinary uneventful day becomes one of joy and celebration. Everyone needs to be recognized and appreciated, and the sheep grow fat."

I know the need to help others came from Dad and Mom, and that has been passed on to the next generation. I have taught my children that if they truly want to be happy, then they need to forget about themselves and learn to serve other people. Recently, one of my daughters told me that her whole day had been taken up with projects, and that none of them were hers. She had spent the entire day helping other people in need: pulling weeds out of an elderly neighbor's garden, taking another friend to a doctor's appointment, picking up a friend to go get a soft drink so that they had someone to talk to, and then bringing dinner to the family across the street, who had just had a new baby. At the end of the day, when she called me just to visit, she said, "Dad, I have been cursed with the Larsen need to serve. I just can't ignore those who need my help. I am exhausted, but I am happy."

Historical

College Softball Game

Being a shepherd means putting the needs of others ahead of your own. Parents are shepherds to their children, and children can easily be shepherds to their friends, as illustrated in the following true story.

"What a moment here in Lakeland, Friday," said an announcer calling the Southeastern University Fire and Grand View Vikings softball game Saturday. "Some things are bigger than the game."

Southeastern softball players Leah Gonzalez and Chapel Cunningham say it was a pressure-filled situation. SEU was ahead 4-1, but the other team had the bases loaded.

Then, the catcher for the Grand View Vikings, Kaitlyn Moses, hit a grand slam.

Between first and second bases, Moses suffered an injury and fell to the ground in pain.

With the win on the line, Cunningham and Gonzalez lifted Moses up and carried her across three bases.

They made sure to tap her onto each base, pushing their opponent ahead in a game they would end up losing.

Moses asked Cunningham and Gonzalez for hugs before being taken to her dugout by her teammates.

"Me and Chapel were like, 'Girl, don't you worry, you deserved that. You hit the ball, injuries happen. We're here for you.'" Gonzales said.

"I just knew it was the right thing to do. Here at Southern they teach us, or especially on our team, they try to tell us to do the right thing that ought to be done. And I knew that that was what we should do, so we didn't really think twice," said Cunningham.

According to the rules, the players said, members of Moses' own team could not touch her or the runs would not count.

"The display of sportsmanship by the Southeastern University softball team speaks volumes to their character, humanity, and greater purpose. The results of their actions caused their team in the game to trail by one run, yet that was of minimal concern to those players in that moment," wrote Grand View softball coach Lou Yacinich in a statement.

"The softball world is small," Gonzales said," and players look out for each other. What would happen if those were one of my girls? I would love for someone on the other team to pick them up and take them around," she said.

The Southern University softball coach, Kayla Watkins, said she was not surprised that her players sprang into action.

"I get feedback on campus all the time about our girls and how they do things. So, for me as a coach, it was just kind of cool because I know that about them. But for others to get to see that in them is kind of cool," she said.

Aired on Channel 8 as supplied
by Southeastern University

CHAPTER 14

"MESSAGE TO GARCIA"

Dependability / Commitment

"There's a way to do it... find it."

Thomas Edison

W E ALL HAVE TRIGGERS in life that evoke an instant response. A certain song may take us back to our first love. A sweet smell can transport us halfway around the world to a beautiful garden we have visited in the past. A word or phrase can stir an emotion, good or bad. With me, "Message to Garcia" is a phrase that triggers within me an immediate sense of frustration and dread. As a child, I hated the phrase.

Growing up, I often heard my father say, "Message to Garcia." This was his directive to one of his children that a job needed to be done, and It was our responsibility to figure out how the task was to be completed. And then do it. He would rarely give us any directions. Instead, he simply offered a word of encouragement. "Son, I know you'll get the job done."

I often felt that "Message to Garcia" was simply a ruse created by my father to get out of performing a task that he personally had no desire to complete. That, or he was trying to teach us the value of trial and error, and the thrill of discovery. I think it was mostly the first. Some days I really hated Garcia. No, I take that back. I hated him every day.

One of the experiences I had with Garcia was the "opportunity" to change the spark plugs in the car. This was probably the first time that I actually believed Dad really didn't know how to do it. "How hard could this be?" I thought. After locating where the spark plugs were, I simply pulled the red wires off and tried to unscrew the plugs. I soon learned that a regular socket wrench would not reach down far enough to unscrew the plug. So, with a bike ride to the local car parts store to procure the correct socket, the rest would be easy. I would just pull the plugs and take another bike ride to the store to get the *right* replacement spark plugs. (I thought all plugs were the same, who knew?) Then I would go back home, put the new plugs in, and the wires back on. Simple! I was to learn over the next four hours that spark plugs had to be gapped and that a thing called a rotor, which allowed the electricity to travel from the plug through those red wires to the engine block, had to be connected in a specific order, which was not sequential, but alternated from side to side. Otherwise, the firing pattern would not work as it was designed. By the end of the day, I had learned a valuable lesson. In the future, Garcia would be better served by simply taking the car to a mechanic.

The only thing I knew about construction, I learned in my eighth-grade woodworking class. Mr. Allen was an excellent teacher, and by the end of the quarter I was able to make one killer shoeshine box. But beyond that one project, my skills were pretty rudimentary. Years later, when I told my family I was leaving a solid and stable job with Pfizer Pharmaceuticals to start my own construction company, I was met with a less-than-enthusiastic response. I knew I wanted to be my own boss, and I loved working with my hands, so it seemed like a perfect fit for me. Enter "Message to Garcia." I didn't know the first thing about operating a construction company. But now it had to be done, and I was the one who would have to do it. Needless to say, the learning curve was pretty steep. I decided to start in the construction industry by installing commercial roofing systems. After looking at all the phases of construction, I realized that the greatest margin for profit, at least for me starting out, would be in commercial roofing. I had no training, and no past experience, but I knew a Larsen could do anything, so off I ran. It was the spring of 1981 and I had no money, so to support my family, I took a job delivering about 400 newspapers early each morning, and at night I did janitorial work, so the days would be free to get the business off the ground. Since there was no advertising budget, I decided to cold call door to door in small rural towns that didn't have a local roofing company. I focused on two small towns in eastern Utah: Roosevelt and Vernal. I would walk the main street, visit all the shops and inquire as to their roofing needs. I was met with zero success. When I started asking the question, "Well, if you don't have any needs, do you know of someone who does?" the answer was unanimous: "The J.C. Penney store down on 45 E. Main in Vernal, Utah."

When I entered the store, I immediately realized why it was notorious. There were five-gallon buckets in every corner of the store just waiting for the next storm to pass through. I asked the manager if I could talk to the owner of the store and was told that it was owned by an old, retired farmer out in the valley named Morgan Merkley. After getting his address, I rode out into the countryside to his farm. After knocking on the door several times, the squeaky screen door slowly opened on a pair of rusty hinges. I saw an old man standing there. He appeared to have passed the age of ninety a few years earlier. He stood about six feet high. In his earlier days he was probably six foot two or better, but time had worn him down a bit. His hair was white and matted down from the effects of a cowboy hat he had worn earlier in the day. He had on old faded blue denim coveralls and a pair of boots that had waded through their fair share of cow pastures. His voice was deep and gruff. After giving me a quick, cursory look, he asked, "What do you want, why are you knocking on my door? Whatever it is your selling, I'm not buying." As he started to close the door, I quickly asked, "Are you the Morgan Merkley that owns the J.C. Penney building in town?" The question stopped the inward swing of the door long enough to allow me just a second to introduce myself and explain the purpose of my visit. When I had finished there was a long, awkward silence as he slowly rubbed his chin and appeared in deep thought. Finally, he spoke. "Young man, follow me."

Off the porch we went and out into the barnyard. We stopped in front of an old structure that Morgan had probably built when he was ten years old. The walls were made from wooden slats that were dark brown, almost black with age, and the roof consisted of several layers of corrugated metal, some of which was missing, and the rest of which was curled and rusted. They obviously had weather close to a century of long, cold winters and dry, hot summers. The structure was twenty feet wide and sixty-eight feet long and nine feet high. The building was still standing, but just barely. The walls were bent and twisted from heavy snowfall. Now the whole structure tilted at about ten degrees. I honestly didn't know how it was still standing.

Morgan then asked me, "Boy, do you know what that is?"

"No sir, I don't," I replied.

"Well, anyone worth his salt knows that's a chicken coop."

"I'm sorry, sir, I should have known that."

"Well, young man," he continued. "If you can put a roof on the coop, then the store is yours."

Message to Garcia: I had no roofing experience.

I was in the middle of a barnyard, and I had no clue how I was going to roof a building that was barely standing. I had two fears: one was that the building would collapse while I was on it and the other was that Morgan would die before I got it done. Two weeks later, I knocked on the same front door, and the same old weathered farmer slowly came out. To his surprise, he saw a new roof on the chicken coop.

After a few colorful phrases, he added, "Young man, I never thought anyone could put a roof on that old coop."

I replied, "Message to Garcia, sir."

"Who?" he asked.

"Never mind," I said. "It's a long story."

"Well, young man, I gave you a promise that if you roofed the chicken coop, that the store would be yours. So go ahead and get it done."

I now had another challenge. How was I going to roof the J.C. Penney store? It was two stories high, in a rural town in the eastern part of the state. I had no equipment to speak of, and I didn't even own a ladder that would reach that high. But that didn't matter. All I was asking for was the opportunity, and it had come. Years later, I drove past that old chicken coop, and to my surprise, it was still standing, I figured the roof was the only thing that was still holding it together.

Historical

Message to Garcia — The story behind the message

Elber Hubbard was the editor of a small magazine called *The Philistine*. In the March issue of 1899, he included an essay entitled, "Message to Garcia" in which he told the story of an incident relating to the Spanish-American war of 1898. The essay became an international sensation, eventually being translated into thirty-seven languages, a book, and two movies, the first one being filmed by Thomas Edison in 1916. The story was given to every Marine and Naval enlistee. The U.S. military had it as required reading for all World War I and World War II soldiers.

"When war broke out between Spain and the United States, it was necessary to communicate quickly with the leader of the insurgents. Garcia was somewhere in the mountain vastness of Cuba, but no one knew where. No mail or telegraph could reach him. The President must secure his cooperation, and quickly.

What to do!

Someone said to the President, 'There's a fellow by the name of Rowan, and he will find Garcia for you, if anybody can.'

(Lieutenant Andrew Summers Rowan was a West Point graduate of 1881.)

Rowan was sent for and given a letter to be delivered to Garcia. How "the fellow by the name of Rowan" took the letter, sealed it up in an oil-skin pouch, strapped it over his heart, in four days landed by night off the coast of Cuba... disappeared into the jungle, and in three weeks came out on the other side of the island, having traversed a hostile country on foot, and having delivered his letter to Garcia, are things I have no special desire now to tell in detail.

The point I wish to make is this: Mckinley gave Rowan a letter to be delivered to Garcia, and Rowan took the letter and did not ask, "Where is he at?"... There is a man whose form should be cast in deathless bronze and the statue placed in every college in the land. It is not book-learning young men need, nor instructions about this or that, but a stiffening of the vertebrae which will cause them to be loyal to a trust, to act promptly, concentrate their energies, and do the thing: "Carry a message to Garcia."

The story in historical context is minor. The war was short-lived and one-sided and arguably unnecessary. But the significance of the essay and the principles it championed were monumental as it influenced young men and women around the world for over half a century.

CHAPTER 15

"IF IT'S WORTH DOING,
IT'S WORTH DOING WELL"

Excellence /
Pride

"No one will ask how long it took to build, they will only ask who built it. Take your time. Do it right."

Aaron Pocock

THE MODEL AIRPLANE P-51 Mustang fighter bomber used in World War II was one I had wanted to add to my collection. It came in a box about two inches high, eight inches wide and about fifteen inches long. It contained three ingredients:

1. The small plastic parts
2. A tube of glue
3. A set of instructions on how to assemble it

The first thing I did was to lay out all the small gray pieces on the kitchen table, open the tube of glue, and then immediately throw away the instructions. Why would I ever need them when there was a perfectly good picture of the finished product on the cover of the box? Instructions were just a waste of time, and often confusing. I continued this same approach for most of the projects I tackled over the next twenty years. It was only after three months of trying to build our first home that I started to understand what Dad had been preaching to me all my life: "If it's worth doing, it's worth doing well." And in order to do it well, I needed to understand how all the individual pieces came together to produce a quality finished product. How could I build a good house if I didn't understand the process? Life is full of ironies. As a child I was too impatient to follow printed plans, and now as a contractor, following a set of plans is not only important, it is imperative. How can you do your best when you don't completely understand how it is to be done?

Was Dad a wealthy man? No. At least not by worldly standards. A highly successful one? Absolutely. He didn't have a lot of money in his bank account, never owned a boat, always bought used cars to drive and lived for sixty-six years in the same small house, a rambler in a tract subdivision. But what he did leave behind was an incredible legacy. His whole life was not spent in accumulating possessions, but rather in accumulating memories, friendships, and acts of kindness and service. He loved people, and they loved him back. Everything he did was 110%. He never did anything halfheartedly. And he always did it enthusiastically. He would often say, "Nothing great was ever achieved without enthusiasm." He would also do it with tremendous energy and with a focus that was single-minded. When he took over the Granite Arts Association, he took a mediocre program and turned it into something amazing. He staged regular cultural events in a city that had a great need for diverse artistic experiences, bringing in the Vienna Boys Choir, world renowned classical guitarist Andres Segovia, pianists Ferrante and Teicher, Royal Winnipeg Ballet, Victor Jory, and others.

When he was given the assignment of being principal of a high school that was old and tired (the building had been there since 1907), the glory days in sports and the arts had long since passed and a sense of camaraderie was all but non-existent. He immediately went to work focusing first on improving school pride. He brought all the old trophies out of the basement, dusted them off and arranged them prominently in the front hallway display case, where everyone entering the school could see them. He encouraged everyone to memorize the school fight song, held pep rallies, and personally participated in school plays, the first being *Show Boat,* where he belted out a rousing solo of *Old Man River*. Dad had absolutely no musical talent, but you could not deny his enthusiastic off-key rendition. It brought the house down. His attitude was always, "Do your best, and be your best, and get involved."

Historical

George Pocock — Known for building the finest racing shells in the world.

In 1935, nine young men from the University of Washington overcame all odds to accomplish an amazing feat. Winning the gold medal in rowing at the Summer Olympics in Berlin, Germany. Their success was due in a large part because of the boat they raced in, a Pocock "Scull Boat." It was the finest racing boat ever built by an Englishman named George Pocock.

George Pocock learned the art of building boats as he worked alongside his father Aaron in a shop on the Thames River in the south of England. There Aaron Pocock built racing sculls for Eaton College. There were never any power tools used. The cutting, plaining, and sanding were all done by hand and the finished product was not only a work of high functionality, but also a work of art. Young George became proficient in building boats and at the same time trained to become an excellent rower himself. In 1907, at age seventeen, his father entered him in a prestigious and professional race at Putney on the Thames River with fifty-eight other entries. George had to build his own boat for the race, which he did out of Norway pine. George ended up winning the race.

> "The sponsors of the race, *The Sportsman* newspaper, had a representative there, who handed me my winner's check for fifty pounds, which I viewed as a small fortune. The next morning's issue of the paper described the race, adding, 'Young Pocock was undoubtedly aided by the excellent ship he utilized.' They didn't say who built it, but that didn't matter. I knew."
>
> *George Pocock*

At age twenty-one, George, along with his older brother Dick, found themselves in Vancouver, Canada, where they were given an order to build two boats for $200 for the Vancouver Rowing Club. They had no shop and no place to stay, so they arranged to rent an old boat shed from the club for $100 a month. They would live on the second floor and use the first floor as their workshop.

> "Conditions were not ideal. Daylight showed through the roof, and wind and rain shuddered through the wide gaps between the wallboards. At low tide, the shed sat on a sloping mud bank, listing twenty-five degrees from bow to stern. When the tide surged back in, the waterlogged timbers on which the structure was built weighed it down and held it fast to the mud. George later described the daily routine: 'The water would rise in the shop while we took refuge in the room above and tried to estimate when the next act of drama would occur. Eventually, with a swish and a roar, the logs would break the mud's hold, and up would come the building, like a surfacing submarine, with water rushing out the doors at each end. Then we would start working again, until the next change of tide.'"

> Daniel Brown,
> *Boys in the Boat*.

Soon after completing the boats for the Vancouver Rowing Club, they were visited by Hiram Conibear from the University of Washington, who wanted the brothers to build boats for the new struggling rowing program on campus. The first of what would become legendary eight-oar racing shells was christened *The Rodgers*. Word of their skills spread rapidly, and before long Stanford University wanted one, and other orders followed. The boat house was no longer big enough to meet the demands, so their shop was then moved to a building on the University of Washington campus.

The idea that a beautiful and superbly built racing shell could come from the west was hard for many to accept. That criticism was for a long time a source of frustration for young George. Then, in 1923, the University of Washington traveled to Poughkeepsie, New York and competed in the National Rowing Championship. The rowing world was shocked when this little-known team from Washington, won the race competing in an unknown Spanish cedar shell built by George Pocock. By 1943, all thirty teams, including colleges such as Cornell, Syracuse, Columbia, Navy, Harvard, and Yale, were all using Pocock racing shells.

George used planks of Spanish cedar for sheathing his boats until 1924, when he switched to western red cedar, which he referred to as "the wood eternal." He found it was lightweight, shrunk very little, was impervious to rot, and less expensive. Some of his boats were still being used fifty years later.

"In the summer of 1963, the University of Washington Board of Rowing Stewards held its Appreciation Night, honoring George as a 'true friend, wise counselor, and world-renowned designer and builder of racing shells.' The accompanying record of his life achievements concluded, 'Let us close with his own words — which in a shell or building it, George Pocock exemplifies — 'If it's worth doing, it's worth doing well.' "

Gordon Newell & Dick Erickson
Ready All!

CHAPTER 16

"HE WHO DANCES HAS TO PAY THE FIDDLER — OR PAY THE FIDDLER FIRST, THEN THE DANCE IS YOURS"

Accountability / Hard Work

"People are always blaming their circumstances for what they are. I don't believe in circumstances. The people who get on in this world are the people who get up and look for the circumstances they want, and if they cannot find them, they make them."

George Bernard Shaw

EVERYONE REMEMBERS THEIR FIRST date. With me it was Junior Prom. I was excited to go, even with a little trepidation. I shall never forget that first lecture from Dad on proper etiquette. "Son, now that you are dating, there are certain rules I will set down for you, and I expect you to abide by every single one, no exceptions."

Rules:

1. "I want you to take your mother with you on every date,"
   Dad said. Horrified, I quickly responded, "You can't be
   serious. Because if Mom has to go, then I hope she has a
   good time with my girlfriend, because there is no way I am
   going to be there." I noticed that Dad's expression was not
   changing. And I was coming to the realization that dating
   was not going to be part of my immediate future. With this
   discussion now over as far as I was concerned, I stood
   up and started to walk out. Dad was not one you could
   treat with any degree of disrespect, so before I cleared the
   door, his deep voice rang out. "Sit down my friend, I'm not
   through here." He always called me *friend* when he was not
   happy with me. He usually referred to me as son, or Brent.
   But when he called me *friend*, I knew I was on the edge,
   and I had better back away quickly. So, I slinked back into
   my chair.

   "Let me finish before you go off in a huff. I am not saying
   your mother has to be there physically. What I am saying
   is this: don't do anything on your date that you would be
   embarrassed doing if your mother was right there watching you. If her presence would cause you any hesitation,
   then whatever it is you're thinking of doing, don't. If you
   would not be ashamed, then fine, go ahead." I am surprised how many dates Mom has been on, or at least her
   image in my mind.

2. Act like a gentleman. Open the car door for her when she is
   getting in and out. Help her with her coat.

3. If you are walking along the side of the road where cars are
   passing by, make sure you put yourself between your date
   and the traffic. (By the way, I have been doing that with my

wife now for over fifty years, and just recently she asked me why. When I explained the reason, she responded, "Oh, I always thought you just liked the thrill of walking on the wild side.")

4. Tell the parents of the girl you're taking out where it is that you are going, who you will be with, what your activities will be, and what time you will have her home by. Then ask for their approval.

   I shall never forget the first time I tried number four. The girl's father was a very intimidating man. After providing her father with my life history, and a list of references, I found my courage waning, along with my mind. "Sir," I blurted out. "What time would you like me home by?" The father tried hard not to smile and then said, "Young man, I don't care what time *you* get home, but my daughter will be home no later than ten o'clock."

5. "If you have dated a young lady for a while, you may want to hold hands," Dad said. "If you really like her, you may want to give her a kiss goodnight as you drop her off on her front porch. But, son, remember the basic principles of economics." I was curious now where all this was going, and what in the world did economics have to do with kissing a girl goodnight? He continued, "Son, there is a basic principle of supply and demand. When there is a great supply of a certain product, then the demand decreases and the value falls. That product becomes cheap. When there is little supply, the demand increases, and the value of the product goes up. So, son, make your kisses extremely valuable."

6. "Always have the girl home at a reasonable hour." Dad said. "I don't care what time you come home, but she is not to be home late." With rule number six, Dad now had my

full attention. All I heard was, "I don't' care what time you come home, but…"

Wow! I was suddenly free with no restrictions. I could stay out all night if I wanted to. What I failed to realize at the time was that dad was never going to change his philosophy "He who dances has to pay the fiddler" did not come with a mulligan, or a do-over, or a "We will let it ride this time." After my first date was safely home, my friends and I spent several hours just hanging out, and when we realized there wasn't much to do at two o'clock in the morning, we all went home to bed. At precisely 5:30 a.m., my father came into my bedroom to wake me up. Not getting any response, he simply poured a cup of cold water on my feet. It was like I had literally been shot. As I bolted out of bed ready for a fight, I was simply met by that six foot six, 320-pound immovable object called "Dad." After I finished yelling and complaining, he simply said, "He who dances has to pay the fiddler. I don't care what time you came home last night, but you will be up now. It is five-thirty in the morning, and it's time to get to work."

By the way, years later, when I had left home and started my own family, I realized that Dad just naturally assumed that I had learned to embrace the practice of getting up at 5:30 a.m. He would often call early in the morning, and the first thing he would ask was, "I'm sorry, did I wake you up?" I was always very competitive, and I never wanted to give him the upper hand, so it was important to sound as if I had been up for hours. It was imperative to get rid of the groggy voice we all start the day with. So, as I ran to answer the phone, I would practice saying, "Hello…hello…hello…," slowly, deeply, and loudly (loudly seemed to work well). Or sometimes high and fast, or I would use a variation on a theme, such as "Top of the morning!" If I had time to practice, it was, "Well, I am great, Dad, and how about you?" (That was always dangerous because the longer the greeting, the higher the probability of letting the sleepy voice slide through.) I never wanted to admit to my father that I was a slacker or that he had one-upped me. When I would return to bed to get up later, at a more humane time, my wife would always ask, "Your dad again?" There is a certain irony to the patterns in life. All these years later the same question is still being asked, just to the next generation down. But now I am the one asking the question, and not Dad: "I'm sorry, son, did I wake you?"

Over the years, I have taken a few of Dad's sayings and reversed their order. Instead of "He who dances has to pay the fiddler," I prefer, "If you want to dance, first pay the fiddler, then the dance is yours." The prevailing attitude today is: "Buy now and pay later." I would rather save now and buy later. I have paid cash for all my cars, and by doing so, I have saved the interest payments and the stress that comes with having to pay off a loan.

The first car we had, just after my wife and I were married, was an old Plymouth Belvedere that had just under 300,000 miles on it. It was painted an ugly beige, and the shifting was done by pushing buttons on the dashboard that resembled buttons on a radio. Not very manly. It ran for two years until it finally died. We repeated the same process of buying old beat-up cars over the next six years. If the car cost $200 and ran for a couple of years, it averaged out to be a car payment of about $8 a month. We had cheap transportation — not flashy, but effective. The difference between the $8 and the $125 we might have been paying on a new car loan was money we could now put into a savings account in the bank. At the end of six years, we had saved enough money to buy a new car outright with no debt. The only times in our married life where we have danced first and then paid the fiddler later, was borrowing money for our college educations and our home.

He who understands interest, earns it. He who doesn't, pays it.

Historical

The Beatles — Considered the greatest rock band with 20 # 1 singles

Those who have a high degree of success in life are those who have also paid the price through hard work and sacrifice.

Tom Brady, professional football quarterback, was always the first man in the practice facility in the morning, and the last man out at night. The result was seven Super Bowls.

Michael Phelps, a competitive swimmer, trained in the pool six hours a day, six days a week, swimming over 50 miles each week. The result was twenty-eight Olympic medals with twenty-three of them being gold.

Yo-Yo Ma, world renowned cellist, practiced five to six hours every day or 10,000 hours every five years. The result was over ninety albums and nineteen Grammy Awards. When Steve Jobs the founder of Apple Inc. was close to death, he asked Yo-Yo Ma to come to his home. Yo-Yo Ma gave him a private performance in his living room, after which Jobs remarked "Your playing is the best argument I've ever heard for the existence of God, because I don't really believe a human can do this"

The Beatles are the most successful band in history, with Paul McCartney's personal wealth totaling over $1.2 billion. How the Beatles became the most successful band ever did not come by happenstance or a lucky break. It came because they first paid the fiddler.

They paid the price long before taking America by storm in February 1964. John Lennon and Paul McCartney started playing together in Liverpool, England seven years earlier in 1957. From humble beginnings to their most notable work, Sgt. Pepper's

Lonely Hearts Club Band, was over ten years. In 1960, as a small struggling band, they were invited to play in clubs in Hamburg, Germany. What made this a critical time in the band's development was that despite poor conditions, the band was forced to play many times all night long.

Concerning their Hamburg experience, John Lennon once said about their experience in Hamburg Germany, "We got better and got more confidence. We couldn't help it with all the experience playing all night long. It was handy then being foreign. We had to try even harder, put our heart and soul into it, to get ourselves over. In Liverpool, we'd only ever done one-hour sessions, and we just used to do our best numbers, the same ones, at every one. In Hamburg, we had to play for eight hours, so we really had to find a new way of playing."

The total in Hamburg was 270 nights in five trips, covering just a little over eighteen months. In total, prior to their first big break in 1964, it is estimated that they played live over 1,200 times.

> "They were no good on stage when they went there (Hamburg), and they were very good when they came back. They learned not only stamina. They had to learn an enormous amount of numbers — cover versions of everything you can think of. Not just rock and roll, a bit of jazz, too. They weren't disciplined on stage at all before that. But when they came back, they sounded like no one else. It was the making of them."
>
> Philip Norman,
> *Shout*

People who have already paid the fiddler can now dance.

Garth Brooks' hit song, "The Dance," was one of his most successful recordings, and contains the following lyrics:

Looking back
on the memory of,
the dance we shared
'neath the stars above.

Holding you,
I held everything.
For a moment,
I was king.

For a moment,
all the world was right.
But how could I have known,
that you'd ever say goodbye.

And now I'm glad I didn't know,
the way it all would end.

I could have missed the pain,
but I'd have had to miss the dance.

To dance requires sacrifice and hard work. But in the end, it is
well worth the journey.

CHAPTER 17

"NO EMPTY CHAIRS"

Priorities / Relationships

"Never in the field of human conflict was so much owed by so many to so few."

Winston Churchill's tribute to those who gave their lives in World War II

FAYE MANWILL PULLED OUT the travel maps and spread them across the kitchen table by the flickering light of a wick-burning lantern. The engine of his 1936 four-door Ford coupe parked just outside the front door was still hot. Faye had just finished a family trip of over 4,000 miles. An excursion that took them to Niagara Falls in upstate New York, and back to their home in the little town of Richfield, Idaho. The year was 1937.

Mom came from this family who loved to travel. They would go on a family trip at the drop of a hat. Dad's family, on the other hand, rarely traveled far from home. As kids growing up, it was obvious who wore the pants when it came time for vacations. With Mom in charge, and with little or no warning, we would find ourselves camping, fishing, visiting a national park, or just taking a drive in the country. A trip to California was a ritual every spring.

We rented a house on the beach in late May or early June before the tourist season started, so we always got a good discount on the rental. Newport Beach was our favorite. To spend the entire day on the beach with my dad, uninterrupted, was treasured time I will always hold dear.

Family and friends are the most important things in life — more important than anything else.

"He who dies with the most toys wins," has never been said by a dying man.. I have found that as we all get older, and we look back upon the lives we have lived, our regrets are never, "I wish I would have spent more time at work," or "I wish I would have made more money so I could have bought more THINGS." But rather, they most always are, "I wish I would have spent more time with my family and with my friends."

My mother realized that any money saved in household expenses could then be used for family excursions. She had been raised as a frugal farm girl and would find creative and unique ways to save money wherever and whenever she could. Planting a garden, extensive canning of fruits and vegetables, sewing clothes for the family, and so on. One of her most outside-the-box ideas came in the summer of 1967. The carpeting in the house was starting to wear out, so instead of replacing it, Mom decided to make her own. Early every morning she would take one of us boys and go dumpster diving behind carpet outlet stores where we would retrieve carpet scraps thrown away by the installers from the night before. (Back then bright-colored shag carpeting was in vogue: bright yellows, flaming reds, sky blues, and florescent greens.) She would then cut the pieces into squares and rectangles. Then, using contact cement, she would glue them right over the old carpeting, resulting in the look of a patchwork quilt with all the colors of the rainbow. We could play all sorts of games on the living room floor. It was probably the biggest Twister game ever constructed. Some people coming to the house would take their shoes off and start jumping from square to square of the same color. Others would look at the carpeting with rolled eyes and a sigh that basically said, "Oh, really." But we kids loved it. Little did we realize that Mom's frugality was what allowed the trip to Disneyland the next spring to occur.

The most difficult experience a parent will ever go through in life is the death of a child. Our son Eric was ten years old when he passed away as a result of a tragic drowning accident. He was, by all accounts, a very gifted child.

His gravesite is in a beautiful little cemetery in a small, somewhat rural town. There are beautiful old trees, some dating back to the summer of 1850, when the first settlers arrived and started to build homes on the American Fork River. In this sacred spot are well-kept gardens with poppies and sunflowers that glow as the first rays of the sun touch the delicate petals, igniting a soft glow in the early morning mist. On the hillside where he rests is the most peaceful view of the nearby snow-covered peaks of the Wasatch Mountains. On his headstone, we wrote the following inscription: "His life is a tender gift that we will hold in our hearts until we can one day hold him again in our arms." I have a strong and abiding belief (faith) that one day we will be together again. It is part of a plan from a Heavenly Father who loves us.

I would, without a moment's hesitation, give up all my worldly possessions — everything I now have and everything I might one day possess — if in exchange I could spend just five minutes with my son to hold him, kiss him, and tell him how much I love him and miss him. I have thought long and hard on those feelings, and I have come to the realization that if this is how I feel about the one who is gone, then what am I doing about my relationship with those that are still here? Following Eric's death, I determined that I would move heaven and earth in order to never miss a significant family event. I have had to cut short work out of town, cancel meetings or postpone other scheduled events in order to attend a dance recital, a track meet, or a school Christmas program. I can always catch up on work later, but I can never go back and recreate a special moment with a child or grandchild that I might have missed.

A friend of mine once said, "I don't understand you. If I had $500, I would spend it on a new coffee table or a new lamp. If you had $500, you would go on a family trip." I took that as a compliment. Years later, he confided to me that, looking back, he would now happily trade the table for the trip. His table was now gone, but my memories and shared experiences with my family will be there forever.

We worked all week in order to have Friday nights and Saturdays free to take mini excursions. Utah is blessed with some spectacular natural resources, including five national parks (Zion, Bryce, Arches, Canyonlands, and Capital Reef) and three national monuments (Timpanogus Cave, Hoovenwep, and Natural Bridges). Other attractions included national recreational areas, Lake Powell, Flaming Gorge, twenty-eight beautiful state parks, national forests, museums, and more. We would bring food from home, and because we were camping, our only expense would be gas. We have always invested in a national parks annual pass, and now that we are over sixty-two years old, our national pass was a one-time $10 charge. It is good for admission into all 459 national sites around the country. This is one of the best deals I have ever come across.

Family ties built through family traditions mean everything.

Historical

Rescue of shipwrecked sailors in Scheveningen, Holland

"I would like to go back in thought to my native Holland where six generations of my father's ancestors lived in the little village of Scheveningen at the seashore. They were fishermen or had other related vocations, like fishing-boat builders, sailmakers, or fishing-net repairmen. Many of them were also involved in the voluntary but hazardous task of lifesaving. They were stouthearted, experienced men who were always ready to man the rowing lifeboats to go on a rescue mission. With every westerly gale that blew, some fishing boats ran into difficulties, and many times the sailors had to cling to the rigging of their stricken ships in a desperate fight to escape inevitable drowning. Year after year the sea claimed it's victims.

"On one occasion during a severe storm, a ship was in distress, and a rowboat went out to rescue the crew of the fishing boat. The waves were enormous, and each of the men at the oars had to give all his strength and energy to reach the unfortunate sailors in the grim darkness of the night and the heavy rainstorm.

"The trip to the wrecked ship was successful, but the rowboat was too small to take the whole crew in one rescue operation. One man had to stay behind on board because there simply was no room for him. When the rescuers made it back to the beach, hundreds of people were waiting for them with torches to guide them in the dreary night. But the same crew could not make the second trip because they were exhausted from their fight with the storm, the winds, the waves, and the sweeping rains. So, the local captain of the Coast Guard asked for volunteers to make a second trip. Among those who stepped forward without hesitation was a nineteen-year-old youth by the name of Hans. With his mother, he had come to the beach in his oilskin clothes to watch the rescue operation.

"When Hans stepped forward, his mother panicked and said, 'Hans, please don't go. Your father died at sea when you were four years old, and your older brother Pete has been reported missing at sea for more than three months now. You are the only son left to me!'"

But Hans said, 'Mom, I feel I have to do it. It is my duty.' And the mother wept and restlessly started pacing the beach when Hans boarded the rowing boat, took the oars, and disappeared into the night.

"After a struggle with the high-going seas that lasted for more than an hour (and to Hans' mother, it seemed an eternity), the rowboat came into sight again. When the rescuers had approached the beach close enough so that the captain of the Coast Guard could reach them by shouting, he cupped his hands around his mouth and called vigorously against the storm, 'Did you save him?'

> "And then the people lighting the sea with their torches saw Hans rise from his rowing bench, and he shouted with all his might, 'Yes! And tell my mother it is my brother, Pete!'"

> Jacob de Jager's address
> given in October 1976

No empty chairs involves the importance of relationship, and why we are motivated to sacrifice for people we may have never met, yet have an innate love for, to inspire the world for good."

In World War II, Winston Churchill the British Prime Minister addressed Parliament. In speaking of the missions being carried out by the British Royal Airforce who's crews were flying deep into German occupied territory on bombing raids aimed at destroying Germanies military power, and where the average age of these young men was 20 and where more than half '70,000' would never return, he paid the following tribute to these brave young men: "Never in the field of human conflict was so much owed by so many to so few."

House of Commons Aug 20, 1940

This song from the play *Les Miserables* always reminds me of the tender feelings I will always have for my son. And that there will be no empty chairs in the Larsen home.

God on high,
hear my prayer.
In my need,
You have always been there.
He is young,
he's afraid.
Let him rest,
Heaven blessed.
Bring him home.
Bring him home.
Bring him home.

He's like the son I might have known,
if God had granted me a son.
The summers die,
one by one,
how soon they fly.
On and on,

and I am old,
and will be gone.

Bring him peace,
bring him joy.
He is young,
he is only a boy.

You can take,
you can give.
Let him be,
let him live.
If I die, let me die.

Let him live.
Bring him home.
Bring him home.
Bring him home.

CHAPTER 18

"THAT WHICH WE PERSIST IN DOING BECOMES EASIER"

Persistence / Goals

"There is no — no. Don't say, 'No, because...' Say, 'Yes, if...'"

Walt Disney

IT WAS NOT A large home, but to me, it was a castle. Since there were four kids to share two bedrooms, I was consigned to the unfinished basement with my older brother. The walls were exposed cold gray concrete, and the ceiling consisted of the floor joists from the rooms above. It was perfect for a young boy. I was the envy of all my friends because I could run wild since there was very little that I could destroy. Even the floor was childproof. It was the ugliest brown tiles that you could imagine, and I am sure they came from a fire sale somewhere. We could ride our bikes, roller skate, and do just about anything that a free-spirited mind could dream up. Our room was decorated about as randomly as any young boy could conceive of. We couldn't ruin the sheetrock since there wasn't any, so we had posters and banners from sports teams taped up everywhere. Each time we went on a vacation, Dad allowed us to buy a cheap souvenir as a reminder of our adventure. On a trip to San Francisco, my brother bought a pendant to add to our random collection back home. It had on it a rendition of the Golden Gate Bridge and Tower Hill, Fisherman's Wharf, and a few other symbols of that beautiful city. On the bottom of the banner was a saying: "They said it couldn't be done. So, he tackled it with a smile, and he couldn't do it either." I absolutely hated that saying. It went against everything I had ever been taught. Because my brother knew how I felt about his new possession, it took a prominent location on the wall right above my bed. And since he was older and tougher than me, there it stayed.

One of my earliest recollections as a young boy was of sitting around the dinner table and listening to lively conversation mingled with a smattering of good-natured bantering. I also remember the first time I complained about Mom serving asparagus. It was tough, looked funny, and tasted strange, and I refused to eat this nasty, weird vegetable. Out of the corner of my eye, I caught my older sister Deanne giving me the "finger across the throat" warning. I had no idea why she was sending me the high sign to stop, until my father reached over with another helping of asparagus and plopped it on my plate. When I started to object, Dad simply said, "Well, son, if you don't like it, then I need to give you a second helping so you can learn to like it." I soon realized that the only way to beat the system was one of three options:

1. Never complain
2. Claim a sudden mysterious illness
3. Learn how to hide the food

I always thought I was so clever by putting the offending vegetable in a napkin, or simply by spreading it out thinner on my plate so it would appear that I had actually eaten some of it. I soon learned that claiming an illness had a profound downside because it meant being confined to my bed for the rest of the night. Trying to hide it also was not very effective. Mom usually was not fooled. I finally realized that the only real solution was to take a small portion and eat it, and pretend it was good. This also came with a potential downside, because it was sometimes followed by a smile of satisfaction from Mom, and also a second helping. The amazing reality was that I eventually came to enjoy asparagus. Eggplant is still a work in progress, but I am afraid that turnips are a lost cause. I have found a solution to this vegetable dilemma. If it is never served at dinner in the first place, I never have to worry about the infamous second helping. I don't know how many times those crazy turnips seem to disappear on their own somewhere between the grocery store and home.

Historical

Panama Canal — The greatest engineering feat in the world

It took a second helping to build the Panama Canal. The first helping under the French was a miserable ordeal that ended in failure. The second helping under the United States was a monumental success.

It's not that the canal became easier to build, but it was definitely a case of our ability to do so having increased through our unrelenting persistence. Building a canal would cut a dangerous trip around the tip of South America of 7,800 miles and three months down to a mere fifty miles and eight hours.

Ferdinand de Lesseps become world famous for being the driving force behind the construction of the Suez Canal, completed in 1869. It connected the Mediterranean and Red Sea. He then convinced his fellow countrymen that it was France's destiny to build a canal through the Isthmus of Panama, connecting the Atlantic Ocean with the Pacific. It would run from Panama City on the Pacific side to Colon on the Atlantic and would stretch fifty miles. Construction started on January 1, 1881 and ended not with success, but with monumental failure nine years later on May 15, 1889.

There were many factors contributing to this disaster. The French underestimated the difficulty of the terrain, climate, working conditions, cost, engineering challenges, supplies, and the transportation and infrastructure needed to support the ongoing construction.

It is estimated that during the nine-year period of French construction, over 22,000 men died either by accidents, malaria, or yellow fever.

Working conditions were deplorable. The rainy season generally lasted from mid-April to mid-December. It would rain almost every day, with annual rainfall of 132 inches. Mudslides were all too common, and high humidity and dense jungles were constant companions.

The men also had to watch out for not only jaguars and other large predatory animals, but also many of the less noticed but equally deadly smaller ones like mosquitoes, ticks, flies, venomous snakes, scorpions, and large spiders, including tarantulas.

> "The effect of the climate on tools, clothing, and everyday personal items was devastating. Anything made of iron or steel turned bright orange with rust. Books, shoes, belts, knapsacks, instrument cases and machete scabbards grew mold overnight. Glued furniture fell apart, and clothes seldom ever dried. Men in the field finished a day drenched to the skin from rain and sweat and had to start again the next morning wearing the same clothes, still as wet as the night before. Without laundry facilities, a clean shirt or fresh pair of trousers were luxuries beyond compare. Panama was 'a hell on earth,' an English traveler on the Panama Railroad once observed."
>
> David McCullough,
> *The Path Between the Seas,*

One of the biggest factors was the mindset of the French engineers. They came highly educated, but rigid in their designs and their implementation. While Americans may not have had the technical expertise, they were very adept at improvising. An American engineer by the name of John Fritz has been quoted as saying, "Now, boys, we have got her done, let's start her up and see why she doesn't work."

Under Teddy Roosevelt's push, the United States acquired the French assets on May 4, 1904, for around $40 million.

John Stevens was appointed as chief engineer on the canal starting in 1905. He understood the need to have the foundation in place first in order to allow the building of the canal to be on a solid footing. "Sharpen the saw before you begin to cut." In his first year working on the canal, John Stevens realized the critical need to improve morale among the workers. He accomplished this by building housing and barracks, mess halls, hospitals and churches, schools, laundry rooms, and clubhouses. He especially put a high priority on health by eradicating yellow fever-carrying mosquitoes. Still, over 5,609 died during the American time on the canal.

His next priority was the actual work itself. He was able to renovate 1,200 structures left by the French and build 1,250 new ones. The cities of Colon and Panama were cleaned up, and facilities responsible for sustaining the work were constructed, including warehouses, piers, and machine shops. The most critical of all was a total overhaul of the Panama Railroad, which was absolutely vital to bringing in supplies. It would also become a seamless "conveyor belt" in removing the excavated dirt.

If the locomotives and cars were not moving efficiently, the work would come to a standstill. He started by ordering in one hundred new locomotives, strengthened bridges, and double tracks with heavier rails. Repair shops and warehouses were built, and a new telephone and telegraph system was installed.

Five thousand men would start work on the project, including steam drill operators, carpenters, plumbers, bricklayers, painters, cooks, blacksmiths, locomotive engineers, iron workers, train engineers, car repairmen, and steam shovel crane men.

One of the biggest game changers came in the acquisition and use of the ninety-five-ton Bucyrus steam shovel. It was three times larger than the shovels used by the French. And it could dig more than five times the amount of dirt. It was capable of excavating eight tons of rock in one single scoop, and was so large it took ten men to operate it.

The canal would become the most expensive undertaking in world history. It started in 1879 and ended thirty-five years later with the first ship going through on August 15, 1914.

The cost to use the canal is based on tonnage, and the most ever paid was by the Queen Elizabeth II, who in 1975 paid $42,077.88. The least ever paid was by Richard Halliburton, who was an author and world traveler. In the 1920s, he swam the length of the canal in daily segments, and because he weighed only 140 pounds, he was only charged thirty-six cents.

CHAPTER 19

"JUST ADD ANOTHER CUP OF WATER TO THE SOUP"

Friendship / Inclusion

"I've heard it said, that people come into our lives for a reason.
Bringing something we must learn, and we are led, to those people who help us most to grow, if we let them.
So much of me, is made of what I learned from you.
You'll be with me, like a handprint on my heart.
And now whatever way our stories end,
I know you have rewritten mine, by being my friend.
But because I knew you, I have been changed for good."

For Good, song from the play, *Wicked*

A BOAT TO WATER SKI behind, and to occasionally do a little fishing from, sounded great. Dad had always promised that one day we would actually build our own cabin cruiser. It was a dream that somehow went the way of many of my dreams. At first, I held onto the idea with great enthusiasm, but as time passed, the dream faded, and the excitement slowly ebbed away and eventually was totally forgotten. Other dreams I thought were within the realm of possibilities included a ten-speed bike, a trampoline, and — when my imagination really ran wild — I even thought of a cabin in the pine-covered Uintah Mountains. Ideally, it would stand next to a small river, or if my imagination really ran amok, I could see it situated on the shores of a small mountain lake where you could watch the fish swimming around your baited hook and occasionally taking a nibble. At night I could imagine the family sitting around a campfire in front of the cabin, and we would roast marshmallows and make s'mores, and gaze up into a star-filled sky where the Milky Way appeared so brilliant that you felt as if you could reach up and touch it with your finger.

I realized that if the dreams of my childhood were to become a reality, I would have to make considerably more money than what a teacher brought home. Dad was an educator, and he worked as hard as anyone I knew to provide for his family. Those who pursue teaching as a profession have no illusions of getting rich. They do it out of a deep love for the profession and realization that their life's work is really one of service to their fellow men. It was never a surprise when we sat down to dinner to find others joining us. Someone from work, a neighbor, or just anyone who needed a friend. Everyone was welcome.

The roast beef was sliced a little thinner, the pieces of cake were cut a little smaller, the lemonade was a little on the watery side, and the plates on the kitchen table were placed a little closer together. Anyone was welcome, regardless of the time of day, or how close to dinner they arrived unannounced. Dad would always say, "Everyone is welcome to join us. All we need to do is just add another cup of water to the soup, to stretch the meal a little farther so that everyone can be fed."

As I got a little older, and hopefully a little wiser, I started to understand what was truly important to Mom and Dad. Life to them was never about the money. Money could buy "things" but "things" never provided more than a temporary source of happiness. The thing that really mattered to them was forgetting about themselves and learning how to serve other people. That is what brought them real joy, and a real purpose to life.

Dad always taught that if you want to be happy, then forget about yourself and learn to serve others. As a result, our home was a very happy place. Mom and Dad would typically donate ten to fifteen hours of their time each week in service to their fellow men.

This attitude was passed on to me in the fact that, when I got married, my wife and I had an open-door policy in our own home. More often than not, I could walk downstairs in the morning and find two or three of our children's friends sleeping on one of the couches in the family room. For years we never even locked our front door, even when we were gone. In June of 1998, we were traveling as a family to California on vacation. One night I called home to collect messages from our answering machine. When the call went through, I was not greeted by the prerecorded machine message, but by an actual voice.

"Who is this?" I asked.

"Oh," came the reply. "It's Aaron." Aaron just happened to be a good friend of our sixteen-year-old son.

"Well, Aaron," I continued. "We're not around right now. We're on vacation."

"Oh, I know," he said. "I was hungry, and since I was just driving by in the area, I decided to stop and get something to eat. I found a steak in the freezer and I'm cooking it up. I hope you don't mind."

"Of course not, Aaron," I replied. "Just make sure you turn the stove off, and the lights are out before you leave."

Daniel, another friend of the boys, was often at our home and felt a part of our family. One day I walked into the living room and noticed something had been changed in our family picture. In the bottom right-hand corner there now appeared a small school picture of Daniel. He felt bad that he had not been present when the photo was taken, so he had, in essence, photoshopped himself in. Years later, when Daniel was married with kids of his own, I received the following letter in the mail.

Brent and Tineke,
JUNE 09, 2013

"I have been meaning to sit down and write this letter for some time now. It has already been so many years since I was more or less living at the Larsen house."

"More than anything, I wanted to write this letter to say thank you. As time moves along, I look back often to my junior high and high school years and think how amazing both of you are. I cannot imagine how many nights I spent at your home, La Dolce Vita, Village Inn, or somewhere else. How often I was around when all you may have wanted was time with just your kids and I ALWAYS felt welcome. I will forever think of and refer to you both as my second parents. I learned so much from your kindness and generosity. Thank you so much."

"The other day, I was out with my kids on a hike up in Provo Canyon, and I could not help but think about times I spent up there with your family. The traditional Saturday breakfast and drive/activity is something I have tried to do with my kids, and I learned about it from you both. I saw parents that were there if their kids needed to talk, and it has shaped how I try to interact with my own children now and (hopefully) in the future. I am sorry I haven't kept in touch over the years. I am sure you can relate to how life gets busy and you can find yourself pulled in a million directions. But know that I think of you often and am grateful for all you have taught me. Thank you for taking (me) in your home, and for being such good and amazing people. I hope all is well for you both. If there is ever anything I can do for you both, please don't hesitate to ask. I love you both."

Take care,
Daniel

A Thanksgiving Story

The smell of turkey hung in the air as everyone was rushing around getting the final touches of Thanksgiving dinner ready. We had our children and their spouses, grandchildren, the parents of one of our sons-in-law, my sister and some of her kids, and few others tossed in for good measure. As we were getting ready to sit down at the tables set up throughout the house, in walked an elderly couple carrying two pies. I had no idea who they were, so I just assumed one of the family members had invited an older couple to come and join us for dinner. I welcomed them in, took their pies into the kitchen and invited them to find a chair at any one of the tables. As we all got seated, I noticed our new guests were looking around with anxious expressions on their faces. When I asked them if everything was okay, they responded, "We don't recognize anyone here." When I offered to introduce the gang, I was met with a simple question: "This is the Jenson's house, right?" "Well, no." I responded. "They live next door." Even though we offered to feed them, they declined our offer, and with red faces — and two beautiful pies in their hands — quickly excused themselves. When my sister asked who they were, I responded, "Oh, I thought you or someone else had just invited them to come along."

Historical

"We Band of Brothers" — St Crispin's Day speech from Shakespeare's play *Henry V*

The phrase "Band of Brothers" was originally penned by Shakespeare in his play *Henry V*, which he wrote around the year 1599. In the play, Henry, the King of England, crosses the English Channel to capture the throne of France, which he believes is rightfully his. This is part of the ongoing Hundred Years' War. Just prior to the battle of Agincourt, when victory seems uncertain, we find the young king dressed in disguise and wandering among his men in camp, just before the battle on the morning of October 25, 1415. As he talks to his men, he laments just how hard it is being a king. After all, the king is only a man. He then inspires his men with the now-famous St. Crispin's speech.

"This day is called the feast of Crispian:
He that outlives this day, and comes safe home,
Will stand a tip-toe when the day is named,
And rouse him at the name of Crispian.
He that shall live this day, and see old age,
Will yearly on the vigil feast his neighbours,
And say 'To-morrow is Saint Crispian:'
Then will he strip his sleeve and show his scars.
And say 'These wounds I had on Crispin's day.'
Old men forget: yet all shall be forgot,
But he'll remember with advantages
What feats he did that day: then shall our names.
Familiar in his mouth as household words
Harry the king, Bedford and Exeter,

Warwick and Talbot, Salisbury and Gloucester,
Be in their flowing cups freshly remember'd.
This story shall the good man teach his son;
And Crispin Crispian shall ne'er go by,
From this day to the ending of the world,
But we in it shall be remember'd;
We few, we happy few, we band of brothers;
For he to-day that sheds his blood with me
Shall be my brother; be he ne'er so vile,
This day shall gentle his condition:
And gentlemen in England now a-bed
Shall think themselves accursed they were not here,
And hold their manhoods cheap whiles any speaks
That fought with us upon Saint Crispin's day."

Stephen Ambrose used the phrase, "Band of Brothers" as the title of his book recounting the heroic exploits of Company E, who were the spear of the assault on the German Army from the time the Allied Forces came ashore in Normandy, France on June 6, 1944, until Hitler was defeated eleven months later in Berlin. The unconditional surrender of Germany occurred on May 8, 1945.

CHAPTER 20

"CALL A SPADE A SPADE"

Honesty / Truthfulness

**"This above all: to thine own self be true,
And it must follow, as the night the day,
Thou canst not then be false to any man."**

Shakespeare

THE SUN WAS OUT. The oaks and maples were displaying their fall wardrobe of brilliant reds, amber yellows and honey golds. The leaves on the quaking aspen were shimmering like a thousand gold coins. Against a rich, penetrating blue sky, the air was crisp. It was the perfect setting for a fall football game. We had high hopes that today would finally be the day we would actually see our son BJ become a star. He had worked hard to perfect the position of quarterback, but it had so far paid little dividends. Week after week, BJ watched from the sidelines as his team went down to defeat. On this beautiful October day, Grandpa John was in the stands to watch his grandson play. My father John was always very candid in his opinions and rarely minced words. He always called it the way he saw it. After the first half ended with BJ still occupying the bench, Grandpa decided that the coach needed some armchair assistance.

So, in his low, deep voice, he bellowed out loud enough for even the team on the other side of the field to hear, "Coach, if you're smart, and you want to win this game, then put in your best quarterback, BJ If you want to lose then stay with the one you have!" I looked over to see a young boy with his head down, absolutely horrified that his grandfather had just put him front and center. The result of the outburst was that BJ sat out the rest of the game and his team lost again. Grandpa continued to attend his grandson's games and continued to make the same armchair calls, and BJ spent the season on the bench. The one bit of critical information missing from Grandpa's assessments was that the quarterback just happened to be the coach's son, and every time Grandpa expressed his opinion, the coach became more adamant that he would never make a change, even if it might have been in the best interest of the team.

Dad had strong opinions, and he usually had little restraint in expressing them. He always called things exactly as he saw them. If something is right, it will always be right, and if it is wrong, it will always be wrong. You can't be someone you're not. Don't call black, white, or bad, good. No amount of sugarcoating can make it different than what it really is. Don't beat around the bush and don't attach a fancy name to something to make it appear different than what it actually is.

While recently traveling in South Carolina, I asked a man if they had any issues with cockroaches, to which he replied that they didn't have any cockroaches. When I questioned his answer, he said, "We don't have cockroaches, we have Palmetto bugs." I quite like the softer sound for an irritating insect.

Today we call it "reality TV." Dad would have called it "choreographed, hyped-up nonsense." We call cars "preowned" and clothing "gently used." Dad called it "secondhand."

"Uncoupling" is a fancy term for separation or divorce, and "alternative facts" are merely lies. "Biogenesis suspension" is doping. In the real estate business, "charming" really means run down or old, "A real fixer-upper" means the property is probably trashed. In the business world, we use such terms as disruptive, action items, layering, distributed cloud, smart- sizing, growth hacks, pain points, and future-proof content. I have no idea what many of these terms even mean. My grandkids use a language I don't even recognize: lit, bop, salty, snatched, flex, stan, and no cap. In today's world, Dad would have been anything but politically correct. He simply told it as he saw it. "You can't be something you are not," he would say. Avatars would have driven him crazy.

Dad always advocated that one should always get all the facts before making any decision or expressing an opinion. On more than one occasion, Dad failed to heed his own advice, in which case an apology may or may not have followed. In a business setting, not having all the right facts can often lead to a financial hit. Sometimes quite a costly one.

The only time Dad refused to express his feelings (calling a spade a spade) usually came when I needed it the most: When I would ask for his advice as to what I should do when faced with a difficult decision. I would ask him, "If you were me, what would you do?" To which he always came back with the same response: "Well, son, since I am not you, then it really doesn't matter what I think, now does it?" He would always argue the fact that, if he gave his opinion, or called it as he saw it, it might influence my decision. And if it was wrong, then I would blame him. He simply refused to take responsibility for my actions. He did, however, provide me with a powerful tool in helping me come to my own conclusions. It was his pro vs. con sheet. It was really quite simple. He would take a piece of paper and draw a line down the middle of the page. On the right side, he would label the column "Pros" and on the left he labeled it "Cons." He would then list under the pros all of the positive aspects, and under the cons, all of the negatives. One side would usually outweigh the other, making the decision a lot clearer.

Take the time and effort to correctly get all the facts in order to call something for what it truly is. One story where two men failed miserably to accurately call a spade a spade occurred in the latter part of the nineteenth century.

Historical

Bonanza Silver Mine and the wild west town of Frisco

In September 1875, James Ryan and Samuel Hawks were working in the Galena Mine in the San Francisco Mountains just west of current day Milford in southern Utah. Being a miner meant long days of sweat and grime in a dark, dangerous, and cramped environment. Most miners were single, and those who were married had no family life. A mining camp was no place for a family. A day in the life of a typical miner was getting up before sunrise in the dark, spending his day shift in the mine, and returning to a run-down cabin or a tent in the dark, only to eat in a crowded dining hall with hundreds of other men in the same squalid living conditions. The life expectancy of a miner in 1875 was only fifty-three years, and if a miner lived beyond that, he was on borrowed time. If he didn't die from a cave-in, then lung disease was at the top of the list.

In 1875, there was a national frenzy. Every adventurous young man had pretty much the same dream: go west, find a vein of precious ore, stake a claim, make a ton of money, move to Denver or San Francisco, buy a large mansion and spend the rest of his life actually living that dream. Spending cold nights living in a tent and eating hard bread and salted pork for dinner seemed a small price to pay for the riches that would follow.

While walking to the mine early one morning, James and Samuel happened to stumble upon a unique rock outcropping. Further investigation by these two men revealed a deposit of silver ore. James and Samuel promptly filed a claim on the find and called it the Bonanza Mine. Neither one of these men had any experience running a business, and they had no backing to purchase the equipment necessary to start a mining operation. Also, they felt that this vein was not what it appeared to be. After all, it was probably a small vein. The only problem was that this find was not an ordinary discovery. (It was not just a plain old spade.) It was a golden shovel — a find of epic proportions. They had failed to call this spade a spade. After five months of digging, they finally sold the claim for $25,000. They thought they were incredibly wealthy. The new owners changed the name of the mine to The Silver Horn Mine and started serious mining operations. Four years later in 1879, the United States Annual Mining Review and Stocks Ledger contained the follow entry: "The Silver Horn Mine is the richest silver mine in the world now being worked." When the mine closed on the morning of February 12, 1885, due to a cave-in, profits from the mine had exceeded $50 million.

It is interesting to note that the boomtown of Frisco that sprung up around the mine became just as famous as the mine itself. Frisco had twenty-three saloons, gambling dens and houses of prostitution. Shootings were a nightly occurrence. In fact, the town contracted with a wagon owner to go through the town each day to pick up the dead bodies. One newspaper account called the town of Frisco "The Wildest Town in the West." The town eventually hired a marshal name Pearson from the town of Pioche, Nevada. His job was to clean up the streets. His policy the first day he arrived was really quite simple. There would be no jails, and there would be no arrests. No bail or appeals. Outlaws were given two choices: get out of town or get shot. His first night on the job he killed six men. The town flourished for ten years and then, in 1885, it disappeared when the mine collapsed from the bottom up.

CHAPTER 21

"MY WORD IS MY BOND"

Integrity

"Integrity is doing the right thing, knowing that nobody's going to know whether you did it or not."

Oprah Winfrey

RUBE LARSEN WAS A cattleman, and he was also my grandfather. To him, the smell of cow manure on his boots was not disgusting but represented the sweet smell of success. He not only raised cattle but also bought and sold them. He had a stockyard and an auction house. His work took him across the western United States: Colorado, Wyoming, Idaho, Montana, New Mexico, and Arizona. He made deals with ranchers and farmers large and small. He often referred to these people as "the salt of the earth." Their word was always their bond, as was his. There were few written contracts, and most deals were settled with a simple handshake. Grandpa was very good at what he did. He could take one look at a cow and tell you exactly what the quality of the beef would be. In 1927, he went into business with two other men, establishing a company outside his expertise, buying and selling sheep. The business lasted less than a year, yet in that time the company had created a fair amount of debt. When the business folded in 1928, his two partners took out bankruptcy, but not Grandpa, He had too much integrity to do the same. He immediately went to all of his creditors and promised that if they would work with him, he would pay back every dollar owed. Not only his, but that of his partners, as well.

Grandpa had a habit of never banking with large institutions. He wanted a more personal experience where he knew the employees and they knew him. So, he chose to open his accounts in small towns around the west. One of his favorite banks was the First State Bank of Salina, located about 150 miles south of Salt Lake. The president of the bank was a very colorful man. Every Friday morning, The president would take a large amount of cash out of the bank vault, put it into the trunk of his car, and for the next three days, he would become a sort of bank on wheels. He traveled to little towns in southern Utah and northern Arizona, Kanab, Fredonia, Hanksville, Loa, all of which either didn't have a bank, or the people of that town didn't like the one they had. He would cash payroll checks, collect deposits, and conduct various other banking services.

In 1938, Grandpa sent his oldest son Lou to buy some cattle from a rancher just outside of Delta, Colorado. Lou inspected the cattle and felt that this was a sound investment. When Lou brought out a bank draft to pay for the cattle, he was met with objections from the rancher. "I don't know you, and I have never met your father. How do I know if this draft is good?" To alleviate his concerns, Lou paid for the long-distance call to the bank in Salina to ask the bank president if the check was good. The response from the president was, "I will personally guarantee any check from Rube Larsen up to a million dollars." That was quite a statement and a huge amount to guarantee, especially in 1938. Grandpa's Integrity was never in question.

This was one of Dad's most quoted "isms." His word was always his bond, and there was never room for compromise. You could move heaven and earth, and he would still refuse to go back on his promises. Once he had made a commitment to someone or something, there was absolutely nothing that could force him to back down.

Grandpa Rube was never quick to make a promise, because he knew that once he said yes, there was no going back, regardless of the consequences. Dad followed suit, and so did I. And I have always expected my children to do the same.

When our youngest son passed away, I went into severe depression. I had a hard time even going out the front door, and for six months could not even get up and go to work. I turned the construction business I owned over to an old and trusted friend who moved up from New Mexico to help run the company. After a while, I started getting calls at home from the companies I had been purchasing supplies from for years. They were inquiring as to why the accounts were in severe delinquency. When I could not get ahold of my friend, I went into the office only to find the computers wiped clean and the bank accounts empty. He had taken everything out of the company and disappeared. This was a severe blow to me. I had the loss of a son and now the apparent loss of my company with no way of supporting my family. The debt incurred during those six months was north of $500,000 with my home as collateral for open accounts.

My friend had allowed the license to lapse, and taxes and insurances and payroll were severely delinquent. My attorney advised me to take out bankruptcy, but I refused. My father and grandfather never did, and so neither would I. I went to all those I owed money to and promised to pay back every penny with interest if they would just work with me. They all did. And five years later, with the debt paid off, all accounts were reopened with a no dollar limit issued. They knew my word was my bond.

I grew up with this philosophy. I honestly believed that this was the norm that everyone adhered to. When I started my construction company, I often would agree on a project and the amount I was to be paid, simply on a handshake. I knew I would complete my part of the agreement and just naturally assumed the other party would do the same. When my sons joined me in the business, they were appalled at the lack of written contracts in the files. "I am a man of my word," I would say. "And I expect the others to be the same." One job I remember was a contract for over $500,000, and there was not a single piece of paper exchanged between me and the client. He trusted me to do a good job, and I trusted him to pay me as we had agreed. I now realize, especially in the litigious world we now live in, that not having a contract would be foolish. To me, it was a much simpler world when I first started in business. That world I miss very much.

Historical

The Go-Getter — A story written by Peter Kyne that tells you how to be one

The Go Getter is the story of a crippled war veteran William E Peck who was seeking employment with a lumber company. The owner, a Mr. Ricks, desperately needed a man to run his Shanghai office. Previous managers had failed miserably. The book was written by Peter B Kyne in 1921

"Please give me a job. I don't care a hoot what it is, provided I can do it. If I can do it, I will do it better than it has ever been done before. If I can't do it, I will quit and save you the embarrassment of firing me."

The old man was impressed, and — going over the heads of all the executives and supervisors — he hired William E Peck. Bill was warned to produce and not get out of line. "The first time you tip a foul, you'll be warned. The second time, you'll get a month-long layoff to think about it. The third time you will be out for keeps."

Peck was given the task of selling a lot of undesirable lumber that the company was stuck with. He was happy to do it. He said, "I can sell anything at fair price." He hit the ball hard. For two months, they saw nothing of him. He sold several boxcar loads of skunk spruce, siding, shingles, Douglas fir, and redwood. He sent orders back to the office almost daily. He sold five new accounts and increased sales dramatically. So impressed was the owner that he thought Bill might be a good man to head up the Shanghai office. But, before a final decision could be made, Bill would have to go throughout the "test."

The "test" was to send Bill on an errand to obtain a very expensive blue vase which had been described to him in detail.

Bill was told to obtain it and deliver it to a stateroom in car seven on the train for Santa Barbara so that Mr. Ricks could take it to his wife for their anniversary. Bill was told the approximate location of the neighborhood — which street, which store, and the window where it could be seen. It was Sunday after 3:00 p.m. when Bill went to find the vase. He went to the area where the vase had been seen, but he searched in vain, street after street. It took two blocks of additional searching in all four directions, and four more blocks before he finally discovered the object of his search. He kicked the door, making an infernal racket, but no one responded. He backed away and read the sign over the door: B. Cohen's Art Shop.

He limped to a hotel, picked up the phone book, and found nineteen B. Cohens. He searched for the art dealer in vain and then dialed all nineteen numbers. He emerged from the phone booth, wringing wet from perspiration. It was 6;00 p.m. and his bad leg was starting to give out on him. Then he had a flash of thought: "Could the name have been spelled differently? Was it Cohen, Cohan, Cohn, Kohn, or Coen?"

He went back to the art shop: It was spelled Cohn's Art Shop. He went back to the phone booth and began calling all the Cohns, On the sixth call, he was lucky and got the right B. Cohn. The cook who answered the phone said that Mr. Cohn was dining at the house of a Mr. Simons in Mill Valley. There were three Mr. Simons, and Bill called all of them before connecting with the right one. Yes, Mr. Cohn was there but who wished to speak to him? Mr. Heck? Mr. Lake? A silence followed. Then the maid returned and said, "Mr. Cohn doesn't know anyone named Mr. Lake and wants to know the nature of the business."

"Tell him Mr. Peck wants to speak to him regarding a matter of grave importance." After a frustrating dialogue, Mr. Cohn came to the phone. Bill told him that he had to have the vase by 7:45 p.m. that night and he needed Mr. Cohn to come back across the bay, open his store, and sell him the vase.

Bill was told to contact Mr. Joost. Again, Bill encountered the same kind of runaround as he tried to find Joost at one of the several country clubs. He could not find Joost.

He borrowed a hammer, then hailed a taxi. He was going back to the store to break the window. But when he reached the shop, there was a policeman standing in front of the store. He left and came back and noticed the sign over the store read B. Cohen's Art Storle. He sat down on a fire hydrant and cursed with rage. His weak leg hurt. The stump on his left arm developed a feeling that his missing hand itched. He took the taxi back to the hotel. Hope springing eternally in his breast, he called Mr. Joost, who then after their conversation had to verify with Mr. Cohn the entire story. If Mr. Kek would just wait at the art store, he would come over if the story was accurate.

At 9:15 p.m., Herman Joost arrived and brought the policeman along with him for protection, just in case. He opened and retrieved lovingly the blue vase. The cost was $2,000. Bill had $10, and Mr. Joost refused a check. Bill called Mr. Skinner from the company and asked to have $2,000 sent down. There was a time lock on the safe and no way to get the money. He tried Mr. Rick's residence to see if he had the money. He had left for Santa Barbara. He tried everything. Finally, he went back to his hotel and got his diamond ring with sapphires set in platinum. It was worth about $2,500. He left it until he could bring the money.

It was too late to catch the train that left at 8:45 p.m. He went to the flying field at Mariner. He got the address of the pilot and awakened him at midnight. They headed south in the moonlight with the vase. An hour and a half later they landed in a field of stubble in the Salinas Valley. He limped to the railroad track, and when the train came, he made a torch, stood between the tracks, and flagged down the train. The train slid to a halt, and the brakeman railed on Bill Peck violently. Bill climbed aboard and said he would purchase a ticket. The brakeman said, "That's right, take advantage of your half portion arm and abuse me. Are you looking for that little old man with the Henry Clay collar and the white muttonchop whiskers?"

"I certainly am."

"Well, he was looking for you just before we left San Francisco. He asked me if I had seen a one-armed man with a box under his good arm. I'll lead you to him."

A prolonged ringing at Mr. Rick's stateroom door brought the old gentleman to the entrance in his nightshirt.

"Very sorry to have to disturb you, Mr. Ricks," said Bill, "But the fact is, there were so many Cohens and Cohns and Cohans, and it was such a job to dig up $2,000, that I failed to connect with you at 7:45 p.m. last night as ordered. It was absolutely impossible for me to accomplish this task in the time limit set; but I was resolved that you would not be disappointed. Here is the vase. The shop wasn't within four blocks of where you thought it was, sir. But I'm sure I found the right vase. It ought to be. It cost enough and was hard enough to get, so it should be a precious gift for your wife or anyone else."

Mr. Ricks stared at Bill Peck as if he were looking at a spook. "By all, that's wonderful!" he murmured. "We changed the sign on you, we stacked the Cohens on you, and we set a policeman to guard the shop to keep you from breaking the window. We made you dig up $2,000 on a Sunday night in a town where you are practically unknown. And while you missed the 8:00 p.m., you overtook it at 2:00 o'clock in the morning and delivered the vase. Come in and rest your poor old game leg, Bill Brakeman. I am much obliged to you."

Bill Peck entered and slumped wearily on the settee.

"So, it was a plan!" he croaked, and his voice trembled with rage. "Well, sir, you're an old man, and you've been good to me; so, I do not begrudge you your little joke. But Mr. Ricks, I can't stand things like I could before I was crippled in the war. My leg hurts and my stump hurts and my heart hurts."

He paused, choking, and the tears of impotent rage filled his eyes.

"You shouldn't treat me that way, sir," he complained. I've been trained not to question orders, even when they seem utterly foolish to me. I've been trained to obey them — on time, if possible; but, if impossible, to obey them anyhow. I've been taught loyalty to my chief, and I'm sorry my chief found it necessary to make a buffoon of me. I haven't had a very good time the past three years, and you can pa-pa-pass your skunk wood and larch rustic and short, odd-length stock to some slacker."

At his point, Mr. Ricks apologized profusely and let Bill know that he had passed a test that only one other out of fifteen had passed, and that the reward was a very highly paid position as the manager of the Shanghai office. By the time Mr. Ricks was through with his apology, Bill Peck had forgotten his rage, but the tears of his recent fury still glistened in his bold blue eyes. "Thank you, sir. I forgive you, and I'll make good in Shanghai."

"I know you will, Bill. Now tell me, son, weren't you tempted to quit when you discovered the almost insuperable obstacles I had placed in your way?"

"Yes sir, I was. I wanted to commit suicide before I had finished telephoning all the Cohens in the world. And when I started on the Cohns, well, it was this way, sir. I just couldn't quit, because that would have been disloyal to a man I once knew."

"Who was he?" Cappy Ricks demanded, and there was awe in his voice.

"He was my brigadier, and he had a brigade motto: 'It shall be done.' When the divisional commander called him and told him to move forward with his brigade and occupy certain territory, our brigadier would say, 'Very well sir. It shall be done.' If any officer in his brigade showed signs of shirking his job because it appeared impossible, the brigadier would just look at him once. And then that officer would remember the motto and go and do his job or die trying.

"The brigadier once sent for me and ordered me to go and get a certain German sniper. I'd been pretty lucky — some days. He opened a map and said to me, 'Here's about where he holes up. Go get him Private Peck.'

"Well, Mr. Ricks, I snapped to it and gave him a rifle salute and said, 'Sir, it shall be done.' I'll never forget the look that man gave me.

"He came down to the hospital to see me after I'd walked into one of the Dustricair 88s. I knew my left wing was a total loss, and I suspected my left leg was about to leave, and I was downhearted and wanted to die.

"He came and bucked me up. He said, 'Why, Private Peck, you aren't half dead. In civilian life you're going to be worth half a dozen live ones, aren't you?' But I was pretty far gone, and I told him I didn't believe it. So, he gave me a hard look and said, 'Private Peck will do his utmost to recover, and as a starter he will smile.'

"Of course, putting it in the form of an order, I had to give him the usual reply as I grinned and said, 'Sir, it shall be done.'

"He was quite a man; sir and his brigade had a soul — his soul."

As William Peck told Mr. Ricks the name of the brigadier, Ricks was visibly startled and said, "The brigadier was a candidate for an important job in my employ, and I gave him the test of the blue vase."

CHAPTER 22

"MY SWEETHEART IS MY QUEEN, AND SHE WILL BE TREATED LIKE ONE"

Love /
Respect

"The best and most beautiful things in the world cannot be seen or even touched. They must be felt with the heart."

Helen Keller

IT WAS A SMALL rural farm in a small peaceful farming community in south-central Idaho where my mother was born and raised. The soil was rich, and the pastures radiated an emerald green in spring and a golden amber hue in autumn. The wheat would gently sway in a slight breeze on a calm summer evening, when the noise of the day had subsided, and a quiet peaceful calm had descended on the land. The air would be filled with the somewhat sweet fragrance of fresh cut alfalfa that would linger long after the sun had set. In a good year, if the rains came, a farmer could coax three crops from his fields before the ground froze in autumn. Regardless of the cash crop, every farmhouse had a small garden within easy reach of the kitchen. In these small plots, the family would grow tomatoes, onions, carrots potatoes, and corn — not for sale, but to be consumed at the family table. It was in this setting that two things would occur: the fresh fruits and vegetables were prepared and eaten, and more importantly, it was where most of the family's interactions occurred.

Plans for the day were laid out in the morning, and a report of the day's activities was given every night. It was a special time to unwind from the demands of the day. Stories great and small were told and retold, often accompanied with laughter, or a challenge from one of the family members as to their authenticity. Every family member was given a set of chores on the farm. They were expected to do their fair share, day in and day out. Complaining and excuses were never tolerated. One of mom's chores, among others, was to collect the eggs from the chickens every morning. As she entered the coop, she was met with the wild flapping of wings and the shrill clucking of the hens. The smell alone was strong enough, but what she really hated was the pecking of the birds as she tried to retrieve the eggs from the nests. The other chores were fine for her, but oh, how she hated collecting those eggs. For the rest of her life, she could never bring herself to eat an egg, regardless of how it was prepared. Sunny side over, scrambled, poached — it didn't matter. The local swimming hole was the irrigation canal down the dusty dirt road from the farmhouse, where on a hot summer day, most of the kids in town could be found either building small rafts to float on or catching frogs that frequented the water there. If you weren't at the canal, you had other options, as well. The banister on the side of the steps of the small library in town provided an excellent slide, be it rather short in duration. And the big tire swing hanging from the old maple tree in the front ward was a source of endless hours of entertainment.

My father always felt that my mother was his sweetheart, and was, in every respect, a queen, and that she was to be treated as one might be expected to treat royalty. It meant that we were never allowed to speak back to our mother, never allowed to raise our voices, or even to say no to her. Dad often said, "No one will ever be allowed to make my sweetheart cry." And, standing six feet six inches high and weighing in at 320 pounds, he was intimidating enough to enforce that simple directive. I never had the desire to ever offend my mother — my life was much too precious to make such an unwise decision. At first, we obeyed Dad's directive concerning Mom out of fear of what Dad might do if we ever broke this cardinal rule. But it didn't take long before we obeyed Dad out of love for this sweet woman. I not only learned respect for my mother because Dad demanded it, and would not tolerate anything less, but I also learned respect for all women. To this day, I cannot stand idly by if someone shows any disrespect towards any woman, young or old.

This lesson has been passed down from generation to generation. My father learned it from his father, and now my sons are learning it from me and passing it on to their sons. Recently, my oldest son, BJ, shared this experience he had with his little four-year-old son, Landon. Landon's mother had asked him to clean up his dishes after dinner, whereupon Landon replied, "No, I don't have to." BJ, upon hearing this, reminded Landon that such a response was not tolerated in their home. He came back with, "I don't care, and you can't make me." Stymied as to how to teach this lesson of respect to a four-year-old, his parents finally hit upon the idea that they needed to teach him on a level he could understand. "Fine, Landon, you don't have to mind me. And I don't have to read you a bedtime story either." Immediately, tears welled up in his eyes. He loved bedtime stories, and the thought of losing this privilege caused a change of heart. "Mom, I'm sorry," he said. And into the sink quickly went the dishes.

One of the sound bits of advice my father passed on to me just before I got married was, "Son, never forget to celebrate important

events in your sweetheart's life: birthdays, Valentine's Day, and —
the granddaddy of them all — your anniversary." Dad had made a
special effort on these days to come up with a meaningful gift that
showed he had put a lot of thought into the occasion. He usually
spent considerable time in acquiring a meaning gift, and in many
cases, made the gift by hand: a jewelry box, a figurine hutch, or
something that showed he really cared, and that the gift was not
just an afterthought. For sixteen years, I was flawless in following
Dad's example. Then, in 1992, the wheels didn't just come off; the
whole wagon fell apart.

I came home late one night and was greeted by my oldest
daughter in the driveway. The first words out of her mouth were
not, "Hi Dad, glad your home," but rather a question: "Dad, what
day is it?" I replied, "Well, Friday, of course."

"No," she continued. "What's the date?"

"Well, it's December 20th." This response was followed by an
awkward silence and one of those not-to-be-repeated comments.

I then continued, "I totally forgot that today was our anniversary.
Liz, do you think that she knows I forgot?" She responded with
one of those wise observations only a daughter can give. "Duh, ya
think? How could she not notice?"

In an attempt to redeem myself, and to try to fool her into
thinking I really had not forgotten, I got back into my truck and
drove downtown to find a gift. Do you know how hard it is to find
a romantic anniversary gift at eleven o'clock at night? The only
store still open at that hour was a grocery store. I finally returned
home at midnight, and with great pageantry, I apologized for
getting home so late on this special day. And to let her know that I
had not forgotten the most important day in our lives, I presented
her with THE GIFT. When she unwrapped her present, I was not
met with a soft, loving smile, but with that look that conveyed
in no uncertain terms, "You have got to be kidding." That green
stuffed dinosaur still sits on the shelf in our closet as a reminder

of my total stupidity. But what else could I have done? It was all that I could find at a grocery store late on a Friday night. By the way, that silly little stuffed dinosaur has been one of the most expensive gifts that I have ever given. Every year, about a week before December 20th, she asks what stuffed animal she is going to get this year. The guilt sets in, and she ends up getting a more expensive present than she normally would have received. It's amazing that she has taken one single gift and has parlayed it into a gold mine.

Historical

"The Letter" — Written by Sullivan Ballou to his wife just before his death in the Civil War

Sullivan Ballou was born March 28, 1829, in Smithfield, Rhode Island. He attended law school in Ballston, New York, became an attorney, and served in the Rhode Island Legislature as Speaker of the House. He married Sarah Shumway in 1855 and had two sons, Edgar and William Sullivan. He was thirty-two when he joined the Union Army in 1861 after the start of the Civil War.

Sullivan penned a tender letter to his sweetheart, dated July 14, 1861.

My very dear Sarah,

"The indications are very strong that we shall move in a few days — perhaps tomorrow. Lest I should not be able to write again, I feel impelled to write a few lines that may fall under your eye when I shall be no more.

I have no misgivings about — or lack of confidence in — the cause I am engaged in, and my courage does not halt or falter. I know how strongly American civilization now leans on the triumph of the government, and how great a debt we owe to those who went before us through the blood and suffering of the revolution, and I am willing — perfectly willing — to lay down all my joys in this life, to help maintain this government, and to pay that debt.

Sarah, my love for you is deathless. It seems to bind me with mighty cables that nothing but omnipotence could break. And yet, my love of country comes over me like a strong wind and bears me irresistibly on with all these claims to the battlefield.

The memories of the blissful moments I have spent with you come creeping over me, and I feel most grateful to God, and to you, that I have enjoyed them for so long. How hard it is for me to give them up and burn to ashes the hopes of future years, when, God willing, we might still have lived and loved together, and seen our sons grow up to honorable manhood around us. I have, I know, but few and small claims upon divine providence, but something whispers to me. Perhaps it is the wafted prayer of my little Edgar, that I shall return to my loved ones unharmed. If I do not, my dear Sarah, never forget how much I love you, and when my last breath escapes me on the battlefield, it will whisper your name. Forgive me my many faults and any pains I have caused you. How thoughtless and foolish I have often times been! How gladly would I wash out with my tears every little spot upon your happiness.

But, oh, Sarah! If the dead can come back to this earth and flit unseen around those they loved, I shall always be near you. In the gladdest days, as in the darkest nights… always, always. And if there be a soft breeze upon your cheek, it shall be my breath. As the cool air fans your throbbing temple, it shall be my spirit passing by. Sarah, do not mourn me dead; think I am gone and wait for thee, for we shall meet again."

It is obvious the tender love Sullivan had for Sarah. She was indeed his queen.

Sullivan Ballou was killed a week later at the first Battle of Bull Run on July 21, 1861. Sarah was twenty-four years old when Sullivan died. She never remarried and died at age 80 in 1917.

ABOUT THE AUTHOR

BRENT WAS A PRODUCT of the fascinating and turbulent decades of the 60s and 70s. He came from a very average middle-class family. Growing up, he would be labeled by society's standards as almost invisible. He was surrounded by incredible role models that greatly influenced his life, including teachers, friends, and most importantly, family. Brent was an Eagle Scout and served a two-year mission for his church in northern England.

He met his future bride in a geology class at the University of Utah and graduated with a B.S. degree in History. Putting himself through school, he worked for First Security State Bank. Brent taught students with reading disabilities at Union Junior High School and history at Alta High School before leaving education to work for Pfizer Pharmaceuticals. Eventually, he started his own highly successful construction company, which now includes three of his sons as part of the family business. He also owns three companies involved in real estate development and acquisition.

Brent's greatest joy comes from his family. He is a proud father to two daughters and five sons, and a contented grandpa to thirty grandchildren, with one great-grandchild on the way. He loves sports, photography, and travel, especially in France, England, Holland, and the inside passage of Alaska. He also enjoys being in the outdoors, and cherishes time at their cabin in the Manti-La Sal Mountains or their condo in the red rock country of southern Utah. He enjoys hiking and rappelling slot canyons in the southwest, and river running, especially the mighty Colorado River. Brent also started the Metra Learning Center and On-line Productions. He played the clarinet in the University of Utah marching and pep bands, and remarkably built his first home with no prior construction experience, which still stands forty-five years later.

Throughout his life, Brent has been driven by the undeniable influence one person can have on generations untold, and the profound lessons taught by a father to his sons and daughters. His life reflects the deep and enduring relationship between a father and his children.

www.ingramcontent.com/pod-product-compliance
Lightning Source LLC
Chambersburg PA
CBHW031509120626
46545CB00005B/1801